RUSSIAN THEORY IS A FANCY

A Compendium: Netaji's Death Controversy

SUMERU

Notion Press

Old No. 38, New No. 6
McNichols Road, Chetpet
Chennai - 600 031

First Published by Notion Press 2019

ISBN 978-1-64587-207-8

**"FREEDOM IS NOT GIVEN,
IT IS TAKEN"**

Dedication

I dedicate this to my mother and father,
Amita and Satyen Roy Chaudhury

Table of Contents

Preface

A Facebook group called 'Netaji's Death Controversy' was set up in 2016 to discuss the findings from the declassified Government files and reliable data from other sources.

Many have requested to bring out a compilation of the findings presented in the group in a book form for ready reference. As a part of that effort, this book has been brought out containing mainly those data related to the 'Russian theory.' The other theories will follow.

The articles are supported by photocopies of original letters, Government documents and Notings. This will enable the readers to go through the original language and cipher themselves the conclusions instead of being fed by the author's version, which is typical of other books on the subject. History lovers and those who like to carry on the research further may find this book with documents useful in their further discussions. This compilation can also act as a reference book to counter the long list of evidence-less stories spread by a section of conspiracy theorists.

The book is not required to be read serially chapter wise. Readers may first go through the Table of Contents page and scan the sections, choose the chapter that interests them most and then reach the page. Likewise, the same process may be followed for the remaining chapters.

Acknowledgements

National Archives of India

Declassified Netaji files, www.netajipapers.gov.in

Declassified CIA files

British Library website

World War II Data Base and Time Line

Clippings from Hindustan Standard, Hindustan Times, The Hindu, One India, DNA,

Clippings from Chicago Daily, Nippon Times, Asahi Evening, China Mail,

Articles from media as mentioned in the respective Chapters

Anirban Mitra, Alak Basuchoudhury and members of the 'Netaji's Death Controversy' Facebook group

Netaji's Death Controversy

Undoubtedly the most charismatic and uncompromising of the top-notch freedom fighters, Netaji Subhas Chandra Bose remains one of India's most revered icons, with every political organisation trying to shine in his reflected glory. In fact, such is his charm on peoples' minds that a section of Indians believe that he is still alive and will return someday to "liberate us from our misery." Therefore, although all major biographies of Netaji have concluded he passed away on the night of 18th August 1945 after being grievously injured at the airplane crash at Taihoku (Taipei) airport, many find this unacceptable. They believe it was a ploy set up by Netaji himself to hoodwink the Allied Forces and reach a safe place to continue his struggle for India's freedom. In addition, many believe that Netaji – a life-long political activist – became a recluse and settled in Northern India. And yet another set is convinced he was betrayed by Nehru and Gandhi (the usual suspects nowadays!) and imprisoned in some Soviet Gulag. Today, it is an undeniable tragedy that these never-ending theories have eclipsed the life and achievements of this 'prince among patriots.' He has been reduced to a mystery-thriller.

Of course, all theories must stand the test of investigation, and in recent years, two incidents allow us to probe them freshly. In 2015, the West Bengal Government released a set of files related to Netaji and his family from the state archives. The Central Government followed soon by their declassification of files from the various central ministries, in January 2016.

In contrast to popular belief, these central files were not the only batch to be released; instead, they were the last lot. GoI had, in fact, released a total of 2,324 files over 3 decades, and has since categorically declared in parliament on 2nd March 2016 that there are no more classified 'Netaji files' in its possession.

To any enthusiastic student of history, these files present a wealth of data which sets the records straight and dismisses rumour mongering that is prevalent on Netaji's death issue.

1

Is the 'Russian Theory' an Afterthought?

One of the most prevalent Netaji's death stories for a long time is that he went to Soviet Russia and died there. But was the story so, right from the beginning?

1945

The first reaction among Indians when the news of Netaji's death in a plane crash at Taihoku, Formosa, came in on 23 August 1945 was: disbelief!

Heartbroken, they found out ways to console themselves.

Some thought this was murder but most believed this to be another escape from the Anglo-Americans. Perhaps, very few took the news as real.

NETAJI IS SOMEWHERE, BUT NOBODY KNOWS WHERE

Initially, word spread that Netaji has gone into hiding to an unknown place and will re-emerge at the opportune time. But people were clueless to express where the unknown place was.

In September '46 Forward Bloc leaders said, "Subhas Chandra Bose is alive and will re-appear at the opportune time for the final revolution in order to free India from the foreign yoke." *(image 1)*

In a public meeting Sarat Bose expressed that though he had no information of Netaji, he believes that Subhas was alive. He also said it would be futile to search for him or to try to secure any news of his whereabouts.

SIMULTANEOUSLY BUT SLOWLY, NETAJI'S 'WHEREABOUTS' STARTED POURING IN

- Chicago Daily News reported on 20.12.45, by Phillips Talbot, that Netaji has been "seen" in many Far Eastern centres *(image 1)*

- Alfred Wagg of Chicago Tribune who visited Taihoku airport in September '45 was reporting to many in India that Netaji was seen in Indochina. Wagg had told this in the presence of then Defence Minister Baldev Singh *(image 2)* and also to ex-Punjab Congress President and ex-State Minister Sardar Niranjan Singh Talib *(image 3)*

- Forward Bloc President Sardul Singh too had said that he received intimation from some important Sikhs, in '45, from Shanghai that Netaji had personally spoken to them *(image 2)*

- Naga leader Angami Phizo who had once enlisted as an INA soldier, too, declared that he met Netaji at Peking in 1952. He even published a photo of him with Netaji *(image 4)*

- Sarat Bose, on another occasion, expressed that he has information that Government of India knows that Netaji is in China.

But Such News Was Interspersed with the Fresh News of Netaji's Death

The same Chicago Daily News reported that Forward Bloc President Sardar Sardul Singh Caveeshar told an audience in late 1946 that "he had learnt 'on good authority' that Netaji was recently shot dead on the Russo-Chinese border by Allied troops. So now, I believe that Netaji is dead." *(image 1)*

- Though Forward Bloc President Caveeshar believed Netaji was dead, his Deputy Thevar went on claiming "he had extensive correspondences with Bose, who is now living in China and is engaged in some mission. Bose will re-emerge when his mission is completed." *(image 5)*

- Thevar further stated 'Bose is alive and is forming an "Asian Liberation Army" in Sinkiang province under the protection of the Chinese Communist authorities to free India from "Anglo-American domination." He had been in contact with Bose for the last 7 years and had met him during a visit to Burma.' *(image 6)*

- This is corroborated by Chandra Singh Rawat, MLA from Garwal, who informed that in Dec. '55–Jan. '56, 3 Garwali soldiers who were declared dead by GoI, appeared in their villages and disclosed that they had come from Sinkiang province where 13,000 Indian soldiers with Netaji were waiting for an opportunity to bring India out of Anglo-American influence! *(image 7)*

- Chitta Basu, too, in his aide-memoire, as late as in 1992 said "rumour persists that he soon took another plane, this time to Yunnan, the then Capital of Communist China. *(image 8)*

- Delhi Congress President Jagdish Kodesia testified to Justice Khosla Commission that in 1951 the Bishop of Dalat (near Saigon) told him that Netaji was with him on the day of the crash and also on the day when it was announced.

- Earlier, in 1953, Debnath Das made public Indian Independence League's investigative report where they mentioned a detailed escape plan chalked out by Netaji after Japan's surrender. "Netaji decided to return to Indian soil. It was decided that he would be dropped somewhere in Assam or in Bengal. In case his arrival on Indian soil direct from SE Asia was not feasible, the alternative plan was that he would proceed to China, preferably to Yunnan for the time being." *(image 9)*

- Samar Guha gave a twist to the disappearance tale by citing 'Jugantar' newspaper of 6.3.69 where a West Bengal Police officer, an ex-army man working in Singapore in 1945, narrated that Netaji did not fly from Taihoku. Instead, he left Singapore in a submarine to an "unknown destination." *(image 10)*

- SM Goswami's information was more colourful *(image 11)*. He said:

  i. In a 1946 broadcast, Bose had said, "I shall be coming to you at the earliest of 1947."

  ii. Sarat Bose told him "all I know of my brother is that he is in North China."

  iii. Bose was taking guerrilla training there and became an adviser to Mao Tse-Tung.

  iv. Netaji had established a heavenly kingdom on the other side of the Himalayas, eastern Tibet is the headquarters.

  v. During the Korean War in 1952, Bose's "Asian Liberation Army" fought under the name of Chinese volunteers where McArthur spotted him and wanted to kill him.

  vi. Bose was in Hanoi since 1953 and was present when Ho Chi Minh took an oath. But he's in Cambodia "now" (while deposing to Justice Khosla Commission).

Goswami later said in 1962, Subhas was distributing pamphlets on the Indochina border and also in Tezpur that the advancing army was not Chinese, but the liberation army commanded by Netaji. Netaji's idea was to capture Assam, surround the whole of East Pakistan and make a sovereign Bengal. But Nehru negotiated with the British and Americans that angered Netaji, and he said, "we are going back."

Goswami was so confident of his declarations that he published a booklet in 1970 claiming that "he was ready to take Parliamentary delegation to the country where Netaji was engaged in a life and death struggle for helping a small country which was now a victim of American aggression." He further reported that Clark Clifford, former US Defence Secretary, "described that among the mighty Vietcong, one complete Division of "Asian Liberation Army" was fighting there under the inspired leadership of a super brain." *(image 12)*

So, after going through recorded statements in the first decade or so after the air crash news, we heard of Netaji being in Far Eastern centres, Indochina, Shanghai, Peking, Sinkiang, Yunnan, North China, China, Korea, Dalat, Hanoi, Cambodia, Burma, Tibet, Assam and Bengal but hardly anyone reported that he was in Soviet Russia!

It will be an interesting exercise to find out from when did the 'Russian theory' start.

Chicago Daily, 20.12.46

1946 Bose Death Report

By PHILLIPS TALBOT

NEW DELHI, December 19, 1946 — His friends have finally let death come to "Netaji" Subhas Chandra Bose, one-time Congress Party president who during the war escaped to Axis territory and became fuehrer of the Japanese-sponsored Free India movement.

According to Japanese, Chinese, British, American and some Indian sources, Bose was killed in a Japanese plane crash in Formosa in August, 1945.

But his large and faithful Indian following refused to acknowledge his ashes. Newspapers reported he had been "seen" in many Far Eastern centers. Top men of the All-India Forward Bloc, founded by Bose, declared only last September:

"Subhas Chandra Bose is alive and will reappear at the opportune time for the final revolution in order to free India from the foreign yoke."

The magic of Bose's name still worked and the Forward Bloc prospered. Now, however, its president, Sardar Sardul Singh Caveeshar, admits he was wrong.

In an ingenious explanation, Caveeshar told an audience he had learned "on good authority" that Netaji was recently shot dead on the Russo-Chinese border by Allied troops.

"So now I believe that Netaji is dead."

(The author is an American journalist and a former Assistant Secretary of State of Near Eastern Affairs under the Kennedy Administration. This is a news report written while he was covering India for the Chicago Daily News from 1946 to 1947.)

(2)

US newsman met Netaji after 1945, says counsel

NEW DELHI, JAN. 29.— Lt. General Shidei and the crew members of the so-called "ill-fated plan" in which Netaji Subhash Bose was reported to have died, were the persons who had "actually taken away Netaji from the danger zone", Mr. Gobinda Mukhoty, counsel for the National Committee assisting the Netaji Inquiry Commission said today, report agencies.

Continuing his arguments before the Commission headed by Justice G. D. Khosla, Mr. Mukhoty contended that these were the people who could have done this job and that was why they had to be declared dead so that the victorious Anglo-Americans could not get at the truth".

Netaji was not involved in an air accident on August 18, 1945 and that as a matter of fact, he was seen by an American correspondent, Mr. Alfred Wagg, in Indo-China much later, Mr. Mukhoty told the Commission quoting the evidence recorded with the commission of Mr. Niranjan Singh Talib, President of the Punjab Pradesh Congress Committee.

Mr. Mukhoty said that the then correspondent of Chicago Tribune had told the witness in the presence of late Defence Minister, Mr. Baldev Singh, that Netaji disappeared into Indo-China and did not die in the crash.

The Counsel said that the Punjab PCC president had also deposed that a former president of the Forward Bloc, Mr. Sardul Singh, had told him that he received intimation from some important Sikhs in Shanghai that Netaji had personally spoken to them much after the reported plane crash.

Hindusthan Standard, 30.1.74

(3)

Khosla Commn : on Waug showing Netaji photos

7.8 Another encounter with Netaji which is alleged to have taken place in 1947 is also related by hearsay evidence. This is the story of Sardar Niranjan Singh Talib (Witness No. 192), who has held high office. He was the President of the Punjab Pradesh Congress Committee, a Deputy Minister, and then a Minister of State and subsequently a Cabinet Minister in the Punjab. His story is that in 1947 he went to the house of Sardar Baldev Singh where he was introduced to one Mr. Wag, an American Military Officer. According to Mr. Talib:

"As soon as Sardar Baldev Singh introduced me to him, he took me to another room and he started showing some photographs of Netaji. He said that Netaji disappeared to Indo-China. He did not die in the crash but he disappeared and he went to Indo-China and he showed me photographs of some cottage where Netaji was standing."

These photographs, according to the witness, were taken after the date of the crash. Wag had been commissioned by an American paper to write a story about Bose. This story was however, never published, and there is nothing to show that Wag's encounter with Bose after the date of the alleged crash was ever given publicity under Wag's signature in any American newspaper. Shri Talib went on to say:

"I wanted to take one of the photos. But suddenly I do not know what happened to him; he took all the photos. He got somewhat suspicious and he stopped further conversation. He doubted something that I may not leak it out."

It is strange that the story which was intended to be published in an American newspaper had to be kept secret. According to Dwijendra Nath Bose the story was related to him by Shri Talib. In any event Shri Talib's story is secondary hearsay evidence and Dwijendra Nath Bose's corroboration is one stage further removed.

(4)

Phizo declared in a statement that he met
Netaji in Peking in 1952

(5)

Riddle of Chandra Bose

By N. S. ANANTH

Over 10 years after the reported death of Subhas Chandra Bose, the Government of India has set up a commission to go thoroughly into the matter of his death. The commission, composed of two of Bose's close associates and his elder brother has now arrived in Tokyo in the course of its inquiries.

Ever since the end of World War II there have been recurrent rumors in India to the effect that Bose has been seen in various places. He has been reported as having been seen in Indian villages, in China, in Russia and elsewhere. The Government of India has often been asked what proof it has that Bose really died as has been reported.

One question which is often raised is why Bose does not show himself if he is alive. A hero's welcome awaits him if he returns to India. According to some people, he can even pose a challenge to Nehru as a leader. His past career does not belie it. Besides, his wife and daughter are still alive in Europe. These factors seem to show that he is indeed dead.

On the other hand, Muthuramalinga Thevar of South India has stated that he has had extensive correspondence with Bose, who according to him, is now living in China and is engaged in some mission. According to Thevar, Bose will re-emerge when his mission is completed.

For a long time, the Government of India did not display any interest in the matter. They accepted Bose's death as settled and left it at that. Last August the First Secretary of the Indian Embassy in Tokyo attended a memorial service held for Bose in the Renkoji Temple in Tokyo.

Last September, Prime Minister Nehru stated in reply to a question by H. V. Kamath on the floor of the Lok Sabha (Lower House of Indian Parliament) "We cannot simply interfere in their (Japan's) territory, more especially also because all the principal witnesses are either

Japanese Government officials or others connected with the Government."

Despite this understandable reluctance, the Indian Government had to bow to the mounting pressure and appoint a commission to inquire into the matter, so great has Bose's stature become.

Bose and his Indian National Army has now grown into legendary proportions in India. The life of this man was such that it could easily pass into legend. The mystery of his reported death was the catalyst which brought it to that stage.

He was born in the holy city of Cuttack on Jan. 23, 1897 to a distinguished family. After a brilliant scholastic career, which was marred by one incident, involving a fight with a British professor on account of the professor's manhandling some Indian students, for which he was suspended from the University for a period of two years, he proceeded to England to study for the Indian Civil Service. After passing the examination, he gave up the Civil Service, the first man to do so, because he felt it repugnant to serve a bureaucracy which held India in bondage. He then re-

Nippon Times
12.5.56

Thevar was having extensive correspondence with Bose who was living in China >>

(6)

Bose Claimed Alive in China

Asahi Evening 23.2.56

AFP
CALCUTTA, Feb. 23—Subhas Chandra Bose, India's wartime anti-allied leader, is alive and is forming an "Asian liberation army" wing in Sinkiang Province under the protection of the Chinese Communist authorities, one of Mr. Bose's lieutenants stated in Calcutta yesterday.

Mr. Bose's lieutenant, M. L. Thevar, deputy chairman of the "Forward Block Party" (founded by Mr. Bose) said he had met Mr. Bose during a visit to Burma.

He said the China-formed "Asian Liberation Army" was intended to free India from "Anglo-American domination." He said he had been in contact with Mr. Bose for the last seven years.

ML Thevar of Netaji's Forward Bloc said
* Netaji is alive &
* forming ASIAN LIBERATION ARMY.
* He met Bose in Burma &
*was in touch with Bose past 7 yrs

(7)

Netaji was in China in 1955-56 !!

It was stated by Shri Chandra Singh Rowat, M.L.A. from GARWAL, before Khosla Commission that some time in December, 1955 or January, 1956, three GARWALI soldiers suddenly and misteriously appeared their villages and stayed there secretaly for few months. They were declared dead by the Goverment of India and their wives were enjoying widow-pension.

They enquired about the activities of Congress and other Political Parties. They disclose that they had come from Sing-kiang Province via Nepal. In SINGKIANG, there were about 13,000 Indian soldiers with Netaji and Netaji was waiting for an opportunity to bring India out of the Anglo-American influence.

(8)

extract from Chitta Bose's aide-memoire

The rumour persists that he soon took another plane, this time to Yenan, the then Capital of Communist China. At that time India was not yet free and Bose could have been hunting for a new possible enemy of England, who would precipitate another war that might collapse the British Empire. World Communism would then be an exccellent candidate.

...,...3/-

-3-

If Bose is still held prisoner in the Communist China, he could be strung as leader of a Red Liberation of India from Capitalism. The most strongly anti-communist Chinese leaders admit that if such an event happened, Indian resistance to China would collapse immediately.

(9)

-7-

extracts from IIL Report of 1953 on Netaji's plan after Jap surrender

who suffered during the war and (d) last though not the least, with the political workers of leaftist tendency.

2. Directives were issued to the effect that the attention of not only the Armed Forces of the Azad Hind Govt. but also of all men combatants or non-combatants, working under the Indian Independence League in East Asia, be focussed on the movement in India in order to strengthen its revolutionary character, culminating in Armed Revolution for India's attainment of freedom. The centre of gravity, it was stressed, lay in India itself The final phase of India's struggle had come and those who wanted to continue to serve the cause through faith and sacrifice must go to India, it was thought by some means or other.

3. Details of approach were developed with regard to our work amongst the three services that existed in India and abroad under the British Indian Government. A detailed plan was ee chalked out to contact the Indian Forces working under the British Flag who would be commissioned to take up the task of occupation in East Asia.

4. Netaji decided to return to Indian soil. It was decided that he was not feasible the alternative plan was that he would proceed to China, preferably to Yennan for the time being.

4. Netaji decided to return to Indian soil. It was decided that he would be dropped somewhere in Assam or in Bengal.

5. In case his arrival on Indian soil direct from South-East Asia was not feasible the alternative plan was that he would proceed to China, preferabley to Yannan for the time being.

6. He ruled out his stay in any part of South East Asia and in Japan proper.

...... contd....7.

(10)

Samar Guha's lt dt. 11.3.69 on submarine voyage

from Singapore has been published in ' Jugantar', a Calcutta daily, on 6.3.69 in column-3, page-50. A retired armyman who claimed to have served the Govt. of India at Singapore during the time of War and now again working in the Police Deptt. of the Govt. of W.Bengal disclosed on the basis of his personal knowledge that Netaji Subhas Chandra Bose did not fly to Taihoke in Formosa in any plane, as reported so far, but instead he along with two Japanese officers left Singapore at the time of surrender of Japan in a Japanese submarine for an unknown destination.

This report should be considered as very important as it throws new light on the whole episode of Netaji's escape. I would request you to make an immediate enquiry about the report and let the House know its finding as an answer to my short notice question sent to you herewith.

I hope you will consider it as a part of our national duty to the greatest revolutionary of India, Netaji Subhas Chandra Bose,

With thanks.

Yours sincerely,

Shri Vidya Charan Shukla,
Minister of State, Home Affairs

(Samar Guha)

(11)

SM Goswami at JKCI

...to ... I think your Lordship has seen the picture in my book. I approached the Chinese Ambassador to identify the person in the picture. He said it was Marshal Lio Po Chen. I was convinced that he remained in Eastern Tibet and organised, and today, Netaji Bose's Asian Liberation Army has got four million soldiers. Mr. Griffith, eminent political commentator, said that in the world there is no army to match them. So simple, so truthful and so much for humanity that I have never seen. Everyone is given four hours of military training, rest of the time is devoted to making shoes, poultry and doing this and that. It is a self-sufficient country. Only raw materials come from China to that country. Netaji has established a heavenly kingdom on the other side of the Himalayas. There are hundreds of feeder roads, jeeps and helicopters. Eastern Tibet is the headquarters. Herr Hitler ran away in a submarine to Japan. He came to Mabu Rock - a 'no man's land' in Burma. In 1962, Subhas Bose was distributing two lakh pamphlets on the border, and on 23rd January in Raigunj, Asansol, Shah Nawaz Khan said when he went to Tezpur he came across a pamphlet which stated that the advancing army was not Chinese but the liberation army commanded by Netaji. Netaji's idea was to capture Assam, go through and surround the whole of East Pakistan and make a sovereign Bengal. But Nehru started negotiations with British and American - help us, help us. They came to his aid with machineries and everything. Subhas felt very annoyed. He said, 'We are going back.' There was unilateral cease fire. Nobody has heard about unilateral cease fire. When the Chinese were advancing and winning what made them change their mind and declare a unilateral cease fire? This is never to be found in the military history of the world for many thousand years. Since then he went back. Pakistanis feel proud that Chinese are behind them but no help was coming in the Indo-Pak conflict and Pakistan got defeated by the hands of General Chaudhuri. Biju Patnaik was given overall charge of NEFA where Netaji came. He asked the Air Force people to bomb the places. They refused, saying that until and unless order came from Delhi, they could not do that. It was connected with Netaji, so they refused. Biju Patnaik went there and bombed the places, and then Netaji gave the order - March. Then they captured Sela Pass, Bomdi-la, and came to Tezpur. Biju Patnaik, as overall commander of NEFA, was asked by Nehru to go to America for purchase of arms and ammunition. It is a very funny thing. Biju is known to me for several years but what knowledge has he got in respect of arms and ammunitions to fight this liberation army? For a single person a plane was chartered. What that plane contained I want to know from the Government. Biju was given a diplomatic visa so that there may not be any question about the contents of the plane. Absolutely desperate, poor man ran everywhere to come to the aid of India. There was refusal, refusal. Netaji was a nightmare for Nehru. While I was presenting my book - Everest - Nehru said, 'Why have you written this book?' I was very much attracted by the Government of India's 'Satyameba Jayate.'

"So, from there finding no place Netaji came to Hanoi when Ho Chi Minh took his oath. Robert Kennedy has already mentioned that he is there. I have omitted to mention one thing. During the Korean war in 1952 this Asian Liberation Army fought under the name of Chinese volunteers and there McArthur saw him and wanted to kill him. He was in Hanoi for 3 years and it was he and Hitler who fought the Americans there. 5 lakhs of soldiers were there in the liberation army - Originally North Vietnam had 20/30 thousand soldiers. America claims that they have killed about 2 lakhs of soldiers. Wherefrom these soldiers came? China or Russia did not give soldiers. They were all from the Asian Liberation Army of Subhas Bose, and so far as I know, the Americans started fighting in Cambodia. He was fighting there and he is in

(12)

NETAJI IN CAMBODIA

Kualampur, 15th May '70— Michael Joseph. Press Reporter of one of the ten client States of America engaged to collect the news of fresh escalating War in Cambodia who recently met at Jakarta in a so-called Asia and Pacific Conference on Cambodia Stated that former U.S. Defence Secretary, Clark Clifford described that among the mighty armies of Viet Cong in Cambodian border, one complete division of Asian Liberation Army fighting there under the inspired leadership of a superman brain, and some of the missing General of World War II and these General are holding very key positions and guide line of Viet Cong ALA and NDLF on a persistent pressure Mr Clifford emphatically refused to disclose the identity of that superman with all of these Generals The above statement was originally in EVENING POST.

NETAJI'S "DEATH"
Centre challenged to conduct fresh probe

From Our Patna Office

JANUARY 7, — Mr. S. M. Goswami, who had undertaken world tour for three times in pursuit of Netaji Subhas Chandra Bose, challenged the Central Government to accede to the request of 350 MPs who urged the Government to conduct a thorough probe afresh into the "alleged death" of Netaji.

Mr. Goswami, who was here on a short visit, is a writer of several books, on Netaji. Some year back he also created some sensation by publishing Netaji's are photographs with Chinese Officials in Indian newspapers. He was also a former Special Officer in Anti corruption Department of the West Bengal Government.

In a Press statement, Mr Goswami said that he was sure that Mrs Gandhi like Mr. Nehru would not accede to the demand for a fresh probe in the "so called" death of Netaji. He said that both of them knew quite well that Netaji was alive and that explained their reluctance for holding an impartial inquiry. Mr. Goswami said that he knew where Netaji was and if Mrs. Gandhi was sincere about the inquiry, he was ready to take Parliamentary delegation to the country where Netaji was engaged in a life and death struggle for helping a small country which was now a victim of American aggression.

Published by S. M. Goswami, 53, Circular Road, Ranchi.

2

The Oft-repeated
"Russia Has Vital Information"

There are some who say Russia has vital information on Netaji's death and the Russians are hiding them. But, unfortunately, their claims are all hearsays.

Russia has repeatedly and consistently clarified since 1992, post dismantling of the communist USSR, that after a "detailed study" of their Archives and Classified files they could find "no information whatsoever" on "the stay of Netaji Subhas Bose on the territory of USSR in 1945 and in subsequent years."

Their letters dated. 8.1.1992; 20.3.1997; 20.3.2003 (a detailed reply) and 6.10.2004 are attached. *(image 1 to 4)*

Whatever mention of Bose they found for the period 1940 to mid-'50s in their Archives and Classified files of

1. RGVA

2. RGASPI

3. GARF

4. RGIA DV

5. FSB (KGB)

6. Min of Defence

7. Russian State Library

8. RGAKFD *(ref image 3 for full form of the initials)*

9. **Personal archives of Eva Yakovlevna Lyusternik and I.V. Stalin**

they've handed them over to India, in particular, a **46 PAGE DOCUMENT FOUND IN FSB FILES**, contents of which was given to Justice Mukherjee Commission, in 2004.

In fact, researchers and social organisations interested in verifying themselves the documents kept in Russian Files on Netaji were given the offer *(ref. letter dated 22.6.2007, image 5)* to work in the Reading Halls of the Archives.

There is no news of any Indian "researcher" availing of the opportunity.

Earlier, on 15.9.2005 *(image 6)*, Justice Mukherjee and the accompanying delegates were given the names, addresses, phone no. and contact persons of the archives located in Moscow, St. Petersburg, Irkutsk and Omsk for their own study.

Prior to that, a decade earlier, in 1995, Yu Kotov in his letter to our Ambassador Ronen Sen categorically stated "we can be sure that Netaji has never set foot on the Russian soil"; "Extensive research carried out…can hardly leave any doubts" *(image 7)*

The letter was accompanied by a detailed note no. 73/YuA; dated 27.10.95 *(image 8)*

Even as late as 2016 and 2017, the Government replied in the parliament on 26.4.16 and 9.3.17, that India had approached Russia and other countries again to retrieve any documents related to Netaji and them, including Russia and except Japan, have responded by saying that all materials on Netaji are available for public in their archives/library.

After all these clarifications and opportunities given to the Mukherjee Commission and to India by the Russians, there is no reason to harp on the 'Russian angle' while remaining silent on getting Japanese files.

The only reason left for a continuance of the 'Russian angle' is to avail the opportunity of communist bashing by abetting the "mystery."

(1)

(rough translation)

Ministry of Foreign Affairs
Russian Federation

No. 2/YuA

The Ministry of Foreign Affairs of the Russian Federation presents its compliments to the Embassy of Republic of India and with reference to the Embassy's Note dated 16 September 1991, has the honour to inform that according to the data in the Central and Republican Archives, no information whatsoever is available on the stay of the former President of Indian National Congress, Netaji Subhash Chandra Bose, in the Soviet Union in 1945 and thereafter.

The Ministry avails itself of this opportunity to renew to the Embassy the assurances of its highest consideration.

Moscow
8 January 1992

Embassy of the
Republic of India
Moscow

Directorate of Foreign Relations
Ministry of Defence of the
Russian Federation

March 20, 1997

N 547

The Directorate of Foreign Relations of the Ministry of Defence of the Russian Federation presents its compliments to you and has the honour to forward herewith the letter of Mr. L. Joychandra Singh addressed a second time to the Central Archives of the Ministry of Defence of the Russian Federation.

In reply to this repeated query, the Central Archives of the Ministry of Defence (CAMD) of the Russian Federation has pointed out that there is no other data relating to the fate of Subhash Chandra Bose besides the information conveyed to you vide letter No.1843 dated October 28, 1996 (enclosing No.2/22672 of the CAMD).

We request you to kindly inform Mr. L. Joychandra Singh of the above reply from the Archives.

The Directorate of Foreign Relations of the Ministry of Defence of the Russian Federation avails itself of this opportunity to renew to the Military Wing of the Embassy of India in Moscow the assurances of its highest consideration.

Military Attache in the
Embassy of the Republic of India
in the Russian Federation

Ministry of Foreign Affairs
Russian Federation

No. 1907/3DA

The Ministry of Foreign Affairs of the Russian Federations presents its compliments to the Embassy of the Republic of India in Moscow and, with reference to the Embassy's note verbale No. SA/10/03 dated 8 January 2003 and the Ministry's note verbale No. 142/3DA dated 28 June, 2001 has the honour to inform you about the following:

A search was conducted for documents related to the fate of S.C.Bose in the following federal archives:

Russian State Military Archive (RGVA), Russian State Archives of Socio-Political History (RGASPI), State Archives of the Russian Federation (GARF), and Russian State Historical Archives of the Far East (RGIA DV). The information requested for was not found in the GARF, RGVA and RGIA DV archives.

Copies of the documents found in the RGIA DV Archives were sent to the Embassy in 2001.

No information has been found about the fate of S.C. Bose in the Central Archives of the Russian FSB, the Central Archives of the Ministry of Defence of the Russian Federation, in the manuscript section of the Russian State Library or in the Russian State Archives of Photographic Documents (RGAKFD).

We would also like to inform that the personnel archives of Eva Yakovlevna Lyusternik were sent after her death to the Russian Academy of Sciences', Institute of Oriental Studies and the open part of the archival material on I.V. Stalin was sent from the archives of the President of the Russian Federation to RGASPI.

The Ministry would like to use this opportunity to renew to the Embassy of the Republic of India the assurances of its highest consideration.

Moscow, 20th March 2003

Embassy of the Republic of India
Moscow

Minist   n Affairs
of the   deration

No. 5954/2ДА

The Ministry of Foreign Affairs of the Russian Federation presents its compliments to the Embassy of the Republic of India in Moscow and, in continuation of Note No. 5538/2ДА dated September 14, 2004, has the honour to inform that information sought on the fate of India's prominent political figure Netaji Subhash Chandra Bose was not found in the Central Archives of the Federal Security Service of Russia.

The Ministry avails of this opportunity to renew to the Embassy the assurances of its highest consideration.

Moscow, October 6, 2004

Embassy of the Republic of India
Moscow

No. 4295/2/DA

The Ministry of Foreign Affairs of the Russian Federation presents its compliments to the Embassy of the Republic of India in the Russian Federation and, in reference to the Note SA/89/07 dated 17th May 2007, has honour to inform the following : -

The documents from Russian archives referred to in the Embassy's note, in particular, handed over in June 2001 for official use exclusively by the Government of India including for the work of the Commission set up by it for the investigation of circumstances related to the disappearance of Netaji Subhash Chandra Bose.

We further inform that the access to materials belong to federal and state archives of the Russian Federation is given with the consent of Federal Agency of Achieves (Rosarchiv), and permission to work in reading halls of agency archives is given by authorities of archives belong to concerned agencies on direct requests by embassies, scientific & research institutions and social organizations.

The Ministry of Foreign Affairs of the Russian Federation avails this opportunity to renew to the Embassy of India in the Russian Federation assurances of its highest consideration.

Moscow, 22 June 2007

Embassy of the Republic of India

**MINISTRY OF FOREIGN AFFAIRS
OF THE RUSSIAN FEDERATION**

No. 5830 /2DA

The Ministry of Foreign Affairs of the Russian Federation presents its compliments to the Embassy of India in the Russian Federation and with reference to the Embassy's Notes No. SA/166/05 of 08 August, No. SA/174/05 of 18 August and No. SA/179/05 and No. SA/180/05 of 26 August this year has the honour to inform as follows :

Justice Mukherjee as a Head of the Delegation, set up by the Government of India to inquire about life of Subhas Chandra Bose pertaining to the period from 1945 onwards, as well as the accompanying delegation will be given access to the documents, kept in the Reading Halls of the Federal and State Archives of the Subjects of the Russian Federation in Moscow, St. Petersburg, Irkutsk and Omsk through the Federal Archives Agency of the Russian Federation. All expenditures related to the arrangements for their visit, air-passage, accommodation, transport and medical insurance etc. should be borne by the Indian side. The Federal Archive Agency requests to inform Mr. M.K. Mukherjee of the addresses of Federal Archives, given below :

1. Russian State Archive for social and political history – 103 821. Moscow, 15, B. Dmitrovka Str. Director – Kiril M. Anderson. Tel. 229 97 26.

2. Russian State Archive of Audio- Photo Documents – 143 400, Moscow Region, Krasnogorsk, 1, Rechnaya Str. Director – Lyudmila P. Zapryagaeva. Tel. 562 14 64, 563 08 45

3. Russian State Archive for Phono Documents, 105 005, Moscow, 3, 2ya Baumanskaya Str. Director – Vladimir A. Kolyada. Tel. 261 13 00

4. Russian State Naval Archive – 191 186, St. Petersburg, 36, Millionnaya Str. Director – Vladimir S. Sobolev, Tel. (812) 312 11 37

The Federal Archives Agency recommends the following for work with the documents of :

- Central State Archive of St. Petersburg – to apply to St. Petersburg Archives Committee (193 015, St. Petersburg, 39, Tavricheskaya Str). Chairman of the Committee – Mr. Anatoly D. Yashkov. Tel. (812) 271 44 55).
- State Archive of Omsk Region – to apply to the Archive Department of the Ministry for State and Legal Development of Omsk Region. Head – Ms. Galina Yu. Borodina (644 099, Omsk, 1, Tretyakova Str.) Tel. (381-2) 25 57 26
- State Archive of Irkutsk Region – to apply to Archive Department of Irkutsk Region. Head – Ms. Nadezhda K. Shestakova (664003 Irkutsk, 36a, Gorkogo Str), Tel. (395-2) 24 06 42.

The Ministry avails itself of this opportunity to renew to the Embassy of the Republic of India the assurances of its highest consideration.

Moscow "15 " September, 2005

EMBASSY OF THE REPUBLIC OF INDIA
Moscow

Covering of letter no. 73/YuA, dt. 27.10.95

H.E. Mr. Ronen Sen
Ambassador of India
to the Russian Federation

Dear Ronen,

Enclosed You will find our note concerning Subhash Chandra Bose. Do believe that we have tried our best to discover any relevant facts.

Unfortunately, I am profoundly distressed being unable to provide any positive information on the subject of not the least importance for the Indian public. Alas, by now it appears that we can be sure that Netaji has never set foot on the Russian soil. Extensive research carried out upon the latest request of Yours can hardly leave any doubts to this effect.

Sincerely Yours,

Yu. Kotov

(Unofficial Transl

Ministry of Foreign Affairs
of the Russian Federation

73/YuA

The Ministry of Foreign Affairs of the Russian Federation presents its compliments to the Embassy of the Republic of India in Moscow and with reference to the Embassy's note No. SA/83/95 dated July 27, 1995, has the honour to state that as a result of the investigations carried out at the Central Archival Collection of the Federal Security Service of Russia, and the Russian Centre for Retention and Perusal of Documents of Modern History, no Information whatsoever has come to light on the stay of Subhash Chandra Bose on the territory of the former USSR in 1945 and in subsequent years.

The Ministry of Foreign Affairs avails itself of this opportunity to renew to the Embassy the assurances of its highest consideration.

Moscow
27 October 1995

Embassy of the Republic of India
Moscow

3

Samar Guha and His Russian Theory

Samar Guha, academician, 3-time Parliamentarian, a Socialist, propagated the 'Russian theory.'

In Nov. 1988, after 'Glasnost' and 'Perestroika,' he wrote a letter (6-page letter attached) to "Comrade" Gorbachev, President of USSR, for unravelling the mystery of the fate of Netaji.

His claims are serialised below along with the questions that come up in the readers' mind:

Claim (1)

a. *"Bose was escorted to Manchuria by Gen. Shedei of the Jap Army."* (pg. 3, para 7 of his letter)

b. *"Subhas Ch Bose arrived at Dairen at 1.30 afternoon on Aug. 23 1945. Bose got into a jeep and proceeded towards Russian territory. After 3 hrs the jeep returned and informed the pilot of the plane who flew back to Tokyo."* (pg. 4, para 11)

Guha gives the source of his claim as: Intelligence report received in Delhi on Dec. 26, 1945 (pg. 3, para 11)

But Guha:

i. Does not disclose which intelligence report is he referring to?

ii. How was he privy to it?

iii. Who verified the report, if at all there is one, to be authentic?

Claim (2)

"The Interpol…published a report in India that Subhas Bose went to Russia after the fall of Japan" (pg. 4, para 12)

Here too, Guha does not say:

    i. When did Interpol "publish" such a report?

    ii. Where is that "published" Interpol report?

Claim (3)

"In Dec. '45 a report said the Governor of Afghan Province 'Khost' has been informed by the Russian Ambassador in Kabul that there are many Congress refugees in Moscow and Bose was included in their number."

*Guha's source for this claim is: "Maradoff, the Russian Vice-Consul General, disclosed in March '46 that Bose is in Russia." (pg. 3, para 10)

Here again, the same questions arise; if Maradoff's report existed,

    i. How was Guha privy to it?

    ii. Who verified the report to be authentic?

Claim (4)

"There is a secret report which says Nehru received a letter from Bose saying that he was in Russia and wanted to escape to India."

*This, Guha claims was sent to the British Viceroy in India by its intelligence during the early part of 1946.

The obvious question that arises is if such a letter existed,

    i. How was Guha privy to it?

    ii. How does he know that it was sent by British intelligence to the British Viceroy?

Claim (5)

"Dr. Radhakrisnan...confided in his close friends Dr. S Das, CU Philosophy Dept. Head, and Dr. RC Majumdar...that he came to know that Bose was kept captive in Stalin's Russia." (pg. 4, para 14)

*Guha's source for this claim is: SM Goswami's deposition in Justice Khosla Commission (1970–74).

This claim could not be established by Goswami, and Justice Khosla rejected it. On this point, Dr. Radhakrisnan sent a written reply to the Commission, "I have read a verbatim report of Sh SM Goswami's statement, which you are good enough to send me. The last time I met Netaji Subhas Chandra Bose was in Darjeeling in the summer of 1940, and I have not made to Sh Goswami any of the statement he has attributed to me" (refer Khosla Commn Report para 4.121).

Claim (6)

A German Jew Engineer, Zerobin, told A. Sarkar, an Indian Engineer, that as a prisoner he met Bose twice in an orientation camp near Siberian-Mongolian border. Bose was there at least until 1961.

*Guha's source for the claim: This, Sarkar told Guha only after leaving Govt service. (Note also the so-called verbatim dialogue Bose had with Zerobin, as quoted by Guha from Sarkar!) (pg. 4–5, para 15)

**Claim (6) is hearsay. It is not evidence.

Claim (7)

Many other reports appeared in the Indian Press about Subhas Bose's presence in Russia. These reports say that Bose was first a free man, but later he was sent to a Siberian concentration camp (pg. 4, para 13)

This Is a Vague and Contradictory Statement

Gorbachev never bothered to reply to such an unsubstantiated and ambiguous letter. Guha sent reminders and also appealed to our President/PM to pursue the case with Gorbachev, but none gave importance to his letter.

ELSEWHERE

Claim (8)

Guha claimed in parliament in 1969 that in the same year a Hindi periodical reported that Netaji had made a broadcast from Radio Moscow on 20.1.67 on 'Tashkent Agreement.'

This claim was also disproved in the parliament. On enquiry, it was found out that at that time among the students who were sent to USSR for further studies, 3 students had the common name 'Subhas Chandra.' One of them made a radio broadcast for a few minutes on 'Tashkent Agreement.' And this bogus claim was made into an XP Question in parliament!

Claim (9)

Indian Express of 27.2.74 reported that Samar Guha asserted in the parliament that "Netaji is still alive."

Here again, there was no mention of any evidence, supporting documents or any lead for investigation.

Claim (10)

Hindusthan Standard of 23.12.75 reported that Guha alleged that several important documents were missing from Defence Ministry file which included a letter written by Netaji to Nehru from Manchuria

Here too, he provided no source of his information or any evidence. Only wild allegations.

Claim (11)

In a letter dated 7.1.90 to PM Chandrashekhar, Guha wrote:

> *"Chinese Govt also are known to have many such reports about Netaji." … "It is also reported that Bose wrote to both Gandhi and Nehru in 1946 from Russia."*

As usual, he provided no tangible source or any verifiable document

Claim (12)

In the same year, in a letter dated 12.5.90 to the President of India, Guha wrote:

> *"According to available reports top secret classified documents on Netaji Subhas and the reports of the plane crash allegedly involving him are lying in the archives of the Governments of Russia, UK, Japan and USA. I would request you to ask the Govt of India to make special investigations to know from these documents what really happened to Netaji."*

By now we all know that Governments of UK, USA, Russia, etc. have declassified all files related to Netaji and all records with them confirm Netaji's death in 1945, more importantly, Japanese and Allied Forces' Reports.

From all the above 12 instances, it can be seen that Guha, apparently, was overconfident and had a dogged view. (In recent times GD Bakshi has taken up his mantle and, same, without establishing any evidence)

PROF. SASAB GUHA
FORMER
MEMBER OF PARLIAMENT
(LOK SABHA)

8/2 CENTRAL PARK
CALCUTTA 700032
INDIA

Comrade Mekhail Gorbachev
President of U S S R
General Secretary of the
CPSU Central Committee
Moscow
U. S. S. R.

November 5/1988

Dear Comrade Gorbachev,

Kindly accept my hearty greetings for the innovation of the new revolutionary concepts of 'Glasnost' and 'Perestroika'. Your bold move will liberate the eclipsed image of the Russian Revolution and create a new hope of moving towards a new horizon of human liberty and progress.

I am a socialist but not a Communist. However, I always shared the views of my leader, Subhas Chandra Bose, the Russian Revolution should be looked upon as the most significant landmark in the history of evolution of human civilization. Our anti-imperialist struggle for national liberation was immensely influenced by the heritage of 1917 Russian Revolution. But the Stalin-era of absolute rigour and repression in Russia raised many questions in the mind of Indian people about the Soviet System.

Your recent crusade for nuclear-arm-free world peace and your daring precepts of 'Glasnost' and 'Perestroika', to remodel the Stalinist polity and economic system of Soviet Russia have created a universal feeling of appreciation and hope all over the world. If your far-sighted move succeeds, it will open a new era of peace, amity and international understanding.

How the Indian people wish that the Nobel peace Prize be presented to you and you be hailed as the Man of Peace and Progress of the world!

While sincerely congratulating you for your policy of 'Openness' I am placing before you an earnest request for opening the mystery about the fate of the greatest revolutionary hero of Indian freedom, Subhas Chandra Bose, whose image is as captivating for the Indian people as that of Mahatma Gandhi.

MEMBER OF PARLIAMENT
(LOK SABHA)

-2-

After fall of Japan on 15th August, 1945, Tokyo Radio reported on 21rd August 1945 that Subhas Chandra Bose, the Head of the State of the Government of Free India, died in a plane crash at Taihoku (Taipei) in Formosa (Taiwan) on 18th August 1945. The report was considered by the British Government and the Indian people as a palpably fake news intended to cover Subhas Chandra Bose's escape to Russia via Manchuria and across the territory of Siberia.

The reasons for the belief that Bose escaped to Russia are following :

1. Subhas Chandra Bose, twice elected President of the Indian National Congress, always considered Soviet Russia as the greatest ally of the struggle for Indian freedom.

2. During the War days Bose tried to establish contact with Stalin through British Communist Party.

3. While escaping from British prison and British India, in January 1941, Bose intended to go to Russia while reaching Kabul but without getting necessary response from Stalin, he had to move to Berlin across the Russian territory in a tactical bid to use Axis Power, the enemy of the British Imperialism, for securing Indian freedom.

4. Although Bose had his collaboration with the Axis Power to wage revolutionary war against British Imperialism for the national liberation of India, he never uttered a word against Russia during the war days nor acted in anyway against Russian interest. When Hitler treacherously attacked Russia, – Bose, who was then in Berlin, did not fear to take immense risk to denouncing it as an 'Imperialist war against Russia', in his letter to Nazi Foreign Minister, Ribbentrop. Bose did not allow his revolutionary army, organised in Germany, to fight against the Russians.

5. After German aggression of Russia, Subhas Bose made an unprecedented 3-month submarine dash from Germany to Singapore to join hands with Japan, because Japan was then at war with the British but it had its friendly tie with Soviet Russia. * (they were never friends. They were at war in 1939. Then, under non-aggression pact)

-3-

6. While waging revolutionary war of Indian Liberation against the British across the eastern border of India, Bose always tried to maintain contact with the Russian leaders through Jacob Malik, - the then Russian Ambassador in Tokyo.

7. Major General Isoda and Col. Tada of the Headquarter of Field Marshall Tarauchi at Saigon, who were entrusted by Japan for ensuring safe escape of Subhas Bose from being arrested by the British Army, admitted before the 'Commission of Inquery about Disappearance of Subhas Chandra Bose' that Japan agreed to Bose's request to air-lift him to Manchuria so that he could take political asylum in Russia by crossing into the Siberian territory. Accordingly, Bose was escorted to Manchuria by Gen. Shedle of the Jap Army.

8. Two months after the report of Bose's death in an aircrash in Taipei, the Home Minister of the British Government in India informed the British Prime Minister Mr. Attlee in a secret report (1945) :

"Subhas Bose might, of course in certain circumstances, be welcomed in Russia. The easiest course would be to leave him where he is and not to ask for his release."

9. During the early part of 1946, a secret report sent to the British Viceroy in India by its intelligence stated :

"There is a secret report which says, Nehru received a letter from Bose saying that he was in Russia and wanted to escape to India."

10. In another secret report to the British Government by its intelligence said :

"Ghulagi malang had been coupling with live Bose in Russia, and in December (1945) a report said the Governor of Afgan Province 'Khost' has been informed by the Russian Ambassador in Kabul that there are many Congress refugees in Moscow and Bose was included in their number. There is little reason for such persons to bring Bose into fabricated stories."

"At the same time views that Russian officers are disclosing or alleging that Bose is in Moscow is supplied in a report received from Teheran. This stated that Maradoff, the Russian Vice-Consul General, disclosed in March (1946) that Bose is in Russia."

11. Another intelligence report received in Delhi on December 26. 1945 said :

MEMBER OF PARLIAMENT
(LOK SABHA)

-4-

"Subhas Chandra Bose arrived at Dairen (in Manchuria) at 1.30 afternoon on August 23, 1945. Bose got into a jeep and proceeded toward Russian territory. After 3 hours the jeep returned and informed pilot of the plane who flew back to Tokyo." (On this day i.e. after Bose's escape to Russia Tokyo Radio reported Bose's death in an air crash at Teipei).

12. The Inter-Pole, an wellknown world secret service published a report in India that Subhas Bose went to Russia after fall of Japan.

13. Many other reports appeared in the Indian press about Subhas Bose's presence in Russia. These reports said that Bose was first a free man in Russia but later he was sent to a Siberian Concentration Camp.

14. Dr. S.Radhakrishnan, who was the second Indian Ambassador in Moscow, confided his close friends Dr. S.Das, then head of Philosophy Deptt. in Calcutta University and Dr. R.C.Majumdar, the most distinguished Indian Historian of his time that he came to know that Bose was kept captive in Stalin's Russia.

15. Recently, I have come across of a very important report about Subhas Bose's presence in Russia in 1961, from an Indian engineer, A.Sarker, of Calcutta. Sarker was sent to Russia 3 times for training in connection with the Heavy Engineering Corporation for manufacturing heavy machinery, set up in collaboration with Russia. Sarker learnt Russian well.

Sarker worked in Machine Building Plant at Gorlovska near the city Donietsk. He came in contact of a German-Jew who was the Deputy Chief of the Plant (Machinostroitelniizavod). His name was D.A.Zerobin, who was earlier an war machine designer in Nazi Germany.

☆ Zerobin told Sarker that he was captured in Berlin after fall of Germany and was sent to a Re-orientation Camp somewhere in Siberia. He was first taken to Siberia by train and thereafter flown to an undisclosed place and then taken to the Orientation Camp. Zerobin surmised that the Camp was somewhere near Siberian-Mongolian boarder.

Zerobin claimed that in this re-orientation camp, meant for political classes for only top foreign politicians and engineers, he met Subhas Bose on two occasions.

...5

-5-

Zerobin could recognise Bose as he saw him earlier in Berlin during the War days. Bose's Headquarter was then in Berlin. Because of the handsome appearance and rare cut-out of the feature of his distinguished personality Zerobin could immediately recognise Bose.

According to Zerobin, Bose was brought to the Camp in a car accompanied by 2 Mongolians, one as his interpreter. Zerobin believed that both the Mongolians were KGB men but it appeared to him that Bose was well looked after.

Zerobin told Bose, "Sir, I met you in Berlin." Bose replied, 'Quite likely'.

Bose asked Zerobin: "What are you doing here?"

Zerobin   : "I don't know what for".

Zerobin again asked Bose, "What is your programme? Are you going back to India?"

Bose : "I expect it to be soon."

While Bose and Zerobin were talking in German, the Mongolian interpreter, intervened saying, 'Not allowed'.

Zerobin never met Bose thereafter in the Camp.

Zerobin while disclosing his meeting with Subhas Bose warned Sarkar that he should not to disclose it while in Russia as it would endanger both.

Sarkar told about the matter to the Second Secretary of the Indian Embassy in Moscow, who also warned him of the dire consequence if he disclosed it to any body.

Sarkar recently told me about Bose's presence in Russia till 1961 in a particular circumstances as he is now out of Government service and believes that Zerobin is now dead. ☆

Comrade Gorbachev! You have taken many bold steps in disclosing many suppressed facts of horror and repression of the Stalin days. You have done great justice to history by rehabilitating Trotsky and Bhukharin and restoring honour to the great scientist, Prof. Sakharov. Inspired by your great liberal policy of 'Glasnost', I would make an appeal - an appeal from the depth of my soul to you - on behalf of the patriotic people of India to reveal all facts about the universally adored hero of the Indian people, Subhas Chandra Bose.

PROF. SAMAR GUHA
FORMER
MEMBER OF PARLIAMENT
(LOK SABHA)

-6-

Stalin might have done injustice to the legendary hero of Indian freedom, but why would you not reveal it now? Bose was a Promethean hero of Indian Revolution who staked everything for the liberation of his motherland and who was always very friendly with Russia. Why shoud you not let the India people know what happened to their entrepid nationalhero? Wein India believe you to be a man of great vision and human feeling. If you let the Indian people know all about the presen of Subhas Bose in Russia, you will win the hearts of millions of millions of the people of India.

When Comrade Brezhnev visited India in november, 1973. I met him in the President's House as the leader of the Socialist Party in the Indian Parliament and gave him a letter seeking informations about Subhas Bose's presence in Russia. The letter was acknowledged but not replied. (A copy of the letter is enclosed).

Considering the poignancy of the issue involved about our greatest national hero, I hope you will excuse me for addressing this long letter to you.

I am eagerly expecting your reply before your visit to India. With warmest regards.

Yours sincerely,

(SAMAR GUHA)
Former leader of the
Socialist Party in Parliament

Encl: As stated.

4

Purabi Roy, Chitta Basu, Koleshnikov

Purabi Roy claims she had been visiting Russia at regular intervals in the 1990s, to do research work on Indo-Soviet relations and also in search of Netaji in the Soviet Union after Aug. 18, 1945. She is another proponent of the Russian theory. She was examined by Justice Mukherjee on her claims based on the statements, documents and names of persons submitted by her (JMCI Report, para 4.10). But the Commission found that records presented by her contained no evidence of Netaji being in that country. The witnesses disavowed the statements about Netaji attributed to them by Roy. The documents in Russian language submitted by Roy when translated were found to have no relevance to her claim. Justice Mukherjee found no merit in the assertion made by her of Netaji's presence in Russia after 18 August 1945 (JMCI Report, para 4.10.9).

Purabi Roy refers to an article written by Koleshnikov. However, the latter could not be examined by Justice Mukherjee as during Commission's visit to Russia he was posted abroad.

Koleshnikov wrote an article in Russian on Netaji's centenary year. The referred article translated into English speaks of all the already prevailing alternatives on Netaji's death/disappearance in the media; discrepancies in Shahnawaz Khan Report, Netaji's possibility of reaching USSR, Stalin-Molotov 'talk,' interned in Gulag, etc. There is nothing in the article as Koleshnikov's own revelation.

In 2016, History Channel aired a programme on Netaji where an interview with Kalashnikov was shown. There too he says nothing definitively and discusses the same stories

Another story goes that Koleshnikov had given some very important writing to Forward Bloc leader **Chitta Basu** in 1996. Chitta Basu died in the last quarter of 1997. He, along with other Left leaders, had gone to Patna in October '97 to attend an anti-Lalu Prasad rally. On his way back he suffered a massive heart attack inside the train, Danapur Xpress, and died. No one suspected any foul play in his sudden death. But later a rumour was floated that with Basu's death the vital document given to him by Koleshnikov got lost.

Looking back at the incident, the said document must have been with Basu for one full year. Had the said writing been a new revelation on Netaji, Forward Bloc would have made the loss a big issue linking to Chitta Basu's death. Nothing of that sort happened those days.

It has been 21 years since then. Koleshnikov is still available. If that document was so important and unknown writing that Roy claims, why has she not got another copy of the original writing from Koleshnikov and showed that to the world? How long will the people be kept telling without evidence that Netaji was in Russia after 18 August 1945?

Another proponent of the 'Russian Theory' was a retired bureaucrat and ex-MP, **Satya Narayan Sinha**. In the course of his giving evidence to Justice Khosla Commission in 1970, he stated:

'A Russian named Kuslov told him in 1949 that he had met Bose in Cell no. 45 of the Yakutusk prison in Siberia. He says he mentioned the matter to Vice President Dr. Radhakrishnan in Jan. 1951, and to Nehru a little later. Dr. Radhakrishnan told him not to meddle in the affair and spoil his career. Nehru's reply was "a sarcastic laugh."'

SM Goswami, another retired bureaucrat, was a champion of the 'Russian Theory.' He gave evidence on 17.11.70 to the same Commission:

"An officer of the Russian army came on tour to India, after about 11 years of stay in the Soviet Union. In the course of his statement at Kapurthala, he informed the press he had an occasion of seeing Netaji at Moscow. He said that he saw Netaji in the best dress and entering Kremlin with high dignitaries on 24th Dec. 1956. On another occasion, he had a personal talk with Netaji. Netaji told him that he was very anxious to return to India, but unfortunately, there was no response from India for necessary arrangements for his return."

Now, when we superimpose the depositions of two, Sinha and Goswami, one of a well-dressed Bose, publicly and openly, going to the Kremlin and the other version on Bose languishing in Cell no. 45 of a prison in Siberia, and compare, one wonders whether Netaji's death is a mystery or flight of fantasy! Incidentally, neither could provide any supporting document/evidence in support of their claims. They were mere hearsays.

5

Gagandeep Bakshi

Gagandeep Bakshi says *(image 1)*:

1. *"Possibly the IB floated the Gumnami Baba theory to appease the Indian masses and cover their trail."*

2. *"Was the Gumnami Baba story an IB plant which we would all like to believe for emotional reasons?"*

to strengthen the supposed charge that *"Nehru fully connived… to get Bose tortured and killed in Siberia"* and *"our IB, bureaucracy collaborated."*

Well, had Nehru connived, then there would have been more reasons for Congress Government to declare Gumnami Baba as Netaji soon after his death. That would set to rest all speculation on Russian angle and absolve Nehru from all suspicion. But the Government did not.

Also note, with all his theories and so much "information," Bakshi did not appear before Sahay Commission to depose that Gumnami Baba was a "plant," "IB floated"! Nay, he would not and could not because all his statements are conjectures. He started with the conspiracy theorists' typical terminology *"Possibly"!*

Maj Gen Gagandeep Bakshi   <u>1</u>
16 hrs

I would like to believe the Gumnami Baba theory. Im afraid the evidence is not clinching. We are certain that Bose reached Manchuria. Viktor Obakumov and Col Utrekhin of Smersh handled his coming and surrunder. He was taken to Omnsk in Siberia where Soviet Govt had moved in wartime and INA had established an embassy of Indian Govt in Exile. from here he made 3 broadcasts- 26 Dec 1945 , 01 Jan 1946 and 19 Feb 1946. These were recorded in Governor of Bengals office in Kolkata. The British now had proof that Netaji was in Russia.They invoked two intelligence sharing / cooperation in secret ops treaties of Nov 1941 and Mar 1944.Stalin had him arrested and sent to Siberia.The British asked for Bose to be kept where he is. They probably sought access to interrogate him in Siberia. This implied TORTURE. To cover up all this the Japanese deception plan was advertised as correct and Bose was declared dead. Dead men do not scream when they are tortured. The Govt of Nehru fully connived with this treachery to get Bose tortured and killed in Siberia.A rival to Nehrus rule was removed. Abakumaov and Utrekhin were later shot by the Soviets. Our IB , our Beauracracy all collaborated. That is why they will never let the truth come out. Possibly the IB floated the Gumnami Baba theory to appease the Indian masses and cover their trail.Bose was the man who got us our freedom. What was done to him was terrible and we are all equally guilty because of our collective silence. Was the Gumnami Baba story an IB plant which we would all like to believe for emotional reasons? Will even this Govt succumb to pressure from its bureaucracy and Intelligence services to safeguard the reputations of their post- independence bosses?

His other claims such as:

3. *"We are certain that Bose reached Manchuria. Viktor Obakumov and Col Utrekhin of Smersh handled his coming and surrender. He was taken to Omnsk";*

4. *"Abakumaov and Utrekhin were later shot by the Soviets. Our IB, our bureaucracy all collaborated."*

5. *"Stalin had him arrested and sent to Siberia. The British asked for Bose to be kept where he is."*

6. *"They (the British) probably sought access to interrogate him in Siberia."*

– all, each, lack evidence.

7. His statement, *"Netaji made 3 broadcasts – 26 Dec. 1945, 01 Jan. 1946 and 19 Feb. 1946. These were recorded in Governor of Bengals office in Kolkata"* is again an unsubstantiated statement. (refer to Chapter 28)

SM Goswami had made a similar deposition to the Justice Khosla Committee *(image 2 and 3)*. There the

i. dates of the imaginary broadcasts were 19 Dec. 1945, 18 Jan. 1946 and 19 Feb. 1946 (not what Bakshi said, except one date)

ii. the supposed recording was done by BBC, London, and not in Kolkata as mentioned by Bakshi.

The script of this imaginary broadcast circulated by Chitta Basu, mentions Netaji addressing the British Prime Minister as *"Prime Minister of England" (image 4)*. Do we have to believe Netaji making such a silly mistake?

This radio broadcast issue is also a big hoax. No newspaper of the time, 1945–46, have ever reported it.

Bakshi's is a smart story as smart as the 'Paris Man' of 1969 photo.

Para 6.48 of Khosla Commn Report

The story of the broadcast by Netaji is described in the following manner:

Goswami: Netaji made three broadcasts. First one was on 19th December, 1945, just after one month.
Commission: Did you listen to this broadcast?
Goswami: No, Sir. It was recorded in B.B.C. and one of my friends, a Bengali gentleman, who was working there, was an officer - he practically told that.
Commission: Have you listened to the playing of the tape?
Goswami: No, it was recorded in B.B.C.
Commission: Do you know what the speech was about?
Goswami: Yes, shall I read it out?
Commission: Did you hear the tape being played?
Goswami: How can I?
Commission: Where did you get this note?
Goswami: It was recorded in B.B.C. London.
Commission: Your Bengali friend had given this story to you?
Goswami: Yes.
Commission: What is the name of this Bengali friend?
Shri Goswami: I hesitate to give the name. He has already lost his service when this broadcast was published in a Bengali paper BHARATBARSA.

>>

Para 6.48 of Khosla Commn Report

Commission: We want to know how far this broadcast is the true broadcast of Netaji. You did not hear it. You have said that you have not heard it yourself. Unless you give the name of your Bengali friend we can not accept this evidence.

Goswami: Sir, the language is sufficient to give proof.

Commission: We cannot accept that. We must have a person who has heard the broadcast himself. Otherwise this evidence is of no value.

Goswami: Frankly speaking, when I showed this broadcast to Radhakrishnan, he told me, well Goswami, I have heard another broadcast, I said, how is it?

Commission: But you did not hear it. You said three broadcasts. What are the others?

Goswami: The other one was on 18th January, 1946 and the third one was on 19th February, 1946 and this is the fateful broadcast that upset the whole thing. Netaji's one mistake of putting one sentence absolutely shocked the British nation.

Commission: The Bengali friend gave you the typed scripts of all the three broadcasts?

Goswami: Yes.

Commission: You can give them to us. We will try to get copies and ask this Bengali friend to come and give evidence.

Goswami: I do not know where he is now.

Commission: So, you cannot help us to trace him.

Goswami: How can I go on chasing a man who may be either in Japan or London or in Switzerland?

Commission: When did he give you copies of the broadcasts?

Goswami: This broadcast, that gentleman of the B.B.C. came on a trip here. He gave the typed copies to his sister who retained it. Then from the sister some gentleman whose name, with your lordship's permission, I should not say because he is in another service and when he gave it to me and after it was published in BHARATBARSA, Magh, 1367 B. S. he lost his job. BHARATBARSA is a monthly magazine."

Chitta Basu :part of aide-memoire on Radio broadcast

-2-

3. NETAJI'S MESSAGE :   FEBRUARY, 1946

" THIS IS SUBHAS CHANDRA BOSE SPEAKING, JAI HIND. IT IS FOR THE THIRD TIME I AM ADDRESSING MY INDIAN BROTHERS AND SISTERS AFTER JAPAN'S SURRENDER.

THE PRIME MINISTER OF ENGLAND IS GOING TO SEND MR. PETHICK LAWRENCE AND TWO OTHER MINISTERS FROM LONDON WITH NO OBJECT IN VIEW OTHER THAN LET THE BRITISH IMPERIALISM A PERMANENT SETTLEMENT FOR ALL MEANS TO SUCK THE TOTAL BLOOD OF INDIA. NOW, AMONG THESE THREE LONDONERS, ONE HAD TO GO BACK FROM INDIA WITH A BAFFLED HEART ONLY A FEW YEARS AGO.

IT IS AS A SORT OF PRECAUTION, I AM ADVISING INDIANS NOT TO PAY ANY HEED TO THESE IMPOSTERS. I AM SURE THAT MR. PETHICK LAWRENCE WILL HAVE TO SUBMIT AN ADEQUATE EXPLANATION FOR ALL THE MISHAPS AND DISASTERS OF INDIA BY THIS TIME. THE UNDERLYING INTENTION OF THIS ENDEAVOUR BY THE THREE IS NOTHING BUT TO SET A NEW TRAP OF DEPENDENCE IN WHICH INDIA MAY FALL VERY SOON. SO MY EARNEST APPEAL TO THE INDIANS IS THAT THEY SHOULD IN NO CASE HEAR THEM BUT CONTINUE REVOLUTION AGAINST WHAT IS CONTRARY TO ACHIEVE

Subramanium Swamy

Netaji treasure was kept by Nehru, alleges Swamy

Hindustan Times Correspondent

BOMBAY, Feb. 8—Demanding immediate reopening of a full inquiry into the death of Netaji Subhash Chandra Bose, Janata MP Subramaniam Swamy today alleged that a portion of the "untraceable" treasure of Netaji had been "appropriated by the former Prime Minister, Mr Nehru, for personal use."

Making this sensational allegation at a Press conference here, Mr Swamy said, "I am saying this with full responsibility and supporting evidence." Most of the persons who know relevant facts are alive and documents are available, he added.

He wants that the Government should immediately seal all files of cipher telegrams maintained in the Indian Embassy at Tokyo and the External Affairs Ministry. The Government should, also, forthwith record the statement of Mr R. K. Nehru. Also, a very reliable emissary of the Prime Minister should contact the concerned ICS officer immediately and record his statement in detail. He added, "I believe this ICS officer to be of high integrity." Mr Swamy said, in view of the time-factor, he felt Netaji was dead. But this inquiry was bound to provide new dimensions to the Netaji story and unmask the true nature of Nehru-Bose relations, he added.

He said that declassified British Government cables in London had mentioned that the vast treasure of jewels and gold donated by overseas Indians to Netaji was "untraceable or missing." He added that he had gone through those cables when he was in London during the emergency.

According to Mr Swamy, some time in Aug. 1952, the Japanese Government communicated to the then Prime Minister of India that it was in possession of some trunks containing gold and diamond ornaments belonging to the INA and wanted to return it. Mr R. K. Nehru, the then Secretary General of the External Affairs Ministry, carried the message to Mr Nehru.

Mr Swamy said that Mr Nehru then had ordered an ICS officer (now retired and living), who was on tour in the US to study agricultural extension programmes, to proceed to Tokyo "for further studies." puzzled, the officer obeyed the directive and reached Tokyo. After a lapse of two months, in Nov. 1952, Mr Nehru sent this officer, via the Indian Ambassador in Tokyo (and now dead) a cipher-cable written "for Mr—only." The decoded telegram read: "YOU SHOULD DEPART TOKYO DIRECT TO DELHI WITH TWO TRUNKS SEALED AND HANDED OVER TO YOU BY THE INDIAN AMBASSADOR AT THE AIRPORT STOP UPON ARRIVAL IN DELHI PLEASE BRING DIRECT TO MY RESIDENCE AND HAND IT TO ME PERSONALLY REPEAT TO ME PERSONALLY."

Accordingly, the ICS officer left by BOAC flight to Delhi with the trunks but the plane developed engine trouble in Hong Kong, Mr Swamy said. At the airport there, the officer contacted the Governor-General who then made special security arrangements for the trunks. Later, the Governor-General sent a cable to the British Foreign Office informing them of the "two mysterious sealed trunks from the Japanese" on way to India.

When the BOAC flight finally landed in Delhi airport, Mr R. K. Nehru was waiting there in the tarmac in his official car. As this officer alighted from the plane, Mr R. K. Nehru accosted him and demanded the custody of the trunks. The officer refused, showing him the copy of the cipher telegram in which Mr Nehru had said, "hand it to me personally."

At this, the officer was made to sit in the official car, and without going through customs formality, he was brought to Mr Nehru's Teen Murti residence. He was ushered into Mr Nehru's private study where the Prime Minister was waiting. Mr Nehru then ordered the seal of the trunks to be broken, and trunks opened.

According to Mr Swamy, it was then, for the first time, the officer saw what the trunks contained—gold and diamond ornaments. The worth of those at that time was approximately Rs 2 crore and Rs 20 crore at the current prices.

He further alleged, "It is my information that all these ornaments were subsequently melted in Allahabad and credited to Mr Jawaharlal Nehru's personal account. Not a word of Mr Bose's treasure was ever heard again."

Mr Swamy said there was widespread suspicion in the country that Mr Nehru was intensely jealous of Netaji and had tried to stall a proper inquiry into his death.

Subramanium Swamy has been telling us over decades that according to *"the papers that exist with us,"* Bose was put in jail by Stalin and later around 1953 was hanged or suffocated to death in Siberia. But the fact is, till date, Swami has not got any such "paper" vetted by the appropriate authority.

In 1978 Swamy told the press, claiming *"full responsibility and supporting evidence,"* that on arrival of INA treasures from Japan after Nov. 1952, Nehru melted all of them in Allahabad and credited to his personal account. Refer 'Hindustan Times' press clipping of 9 Feb. 1978, attached.

And, in this case, too, he has placed no 'supporting evidence' with the Court or the Government in the past 40 years to take any follow-up action on his charges. His is also just big talk.

On the other hand, declassified records show that the Treasures came to India in 1951 (not in 1952, as mentioned by Swami) and was sent to the National Museum. Shahnawaz Committee members checked them in 1956, and again later some MPs checked them during Morarji Desai's premiership.

7

Deliberate Effort to Spoil
India-Russia Relations

Contrary to what some Indian conspiracy theorists clamour, Prof. Grigori G. Kotovsky, Senior Fellow of Moscow's Inst. of Oriental Studies, had said that Russian scholars had gone into all the documents pertaining to Bose in the Soviet Government and KGB archives but could not find a single line indicating Bose's presence in the Soviet Union in 1945 or thereafter. He said that the persistent rumours about Bose's escape to the Soviet Union are *deliberate efforts by some forces to spoil the present day India-Russia relations.*

He said, after Bose's escape from Calcutta and spending some time in Moscow, Bose realised that nothing would come out of his contacts with the Soviet Government and the CPSU. According to Kotovsky, Stalin decided against helping Bose to avoid diplomatic problems with the UK and other western powers which were then at war with Hitler. They could not openly support Bose. Yet, Stalin ensured Bose travel safely to Berlin.

HT FOLLOW-UP

Netaji did not escape to Russia in 1945, says scholar

Apratim Mukarji
New Delhi, March 6

RUSSIAN SCHOLARS are absolutely certain that Netaji Subhash Chandra Bose never escaped to the Soviet Union after the plane crash at Taihoku airport in 1945.

Deputy Co-Chairman of the Indo-Russian Joint Commission for Cooperation in Social Sciences, Senior Fellow of Moscow's Institute of Oriental Studies and a Nehru Award winner Prof. Grigori G.Kotovsky told the *Hindustan Times* today that Russian scholars had gone into all the documents pertaining to Bose in the Soviet Government and KGB archives but could not find a single line indicating his presence in the Soviet Union in 1945.

The eminent Russian scholar who is here to participate in the 25th anniversary of the Joint Commission, said that the persistent rumours about Bose's escape to the Soviet Union and incarceration in a Soviet prison were "deliberate efforts by some forces to spoil the present day India-Russia relations."

Prof. Kotovsky said the Soviet archives revealed that Bose had first tried to enlist Soviet military assistance to liberate India from the British.

After escaping to Kabul from Calcutta in 1940, he obtained a Soviet visa from the Soviet Embassy in the Afghan capital to travel to Moscow via Tashkent.

But after spending sometime in Moscow, he realised that nothing would come out of his contacts with the Soviet Government and the Communist Party of the Soviet Union.

He then followed the well-established trail of Indian leftists and landed in Germany.

According to Prof. Kotovsky,

Stalin decided against helping Bose because this would have created problems with the Western powers, especially the UK, which were then at war with Hitler.

"The Soviet Government and the CPSU could not openly support Bose for the complicated situation in Europe. But they helped him to travel to Germany," he said.

At the same time, Stalin ensured that Bose travelled to Berlin safely without inviting the attention of Western intelligence.

On his part, Bose persuaded Hitler not to send Indian prisoners-of-war, taken by German troops in the European theatre, to the Eastern Front.

According to Prof. Kotovsky, all these details were brought out two years ago by a scholar of the Institute of Oriental Studies in a journal *Africa and Asia Today*.

HT 7.3.2001

8

Netaji's Last Letter
to the Soviet Union

Netaji was looking for additional support from the Soviet Union. On 20 Nov. 1944, he wrote a letter to the Soviet Embassy in Tokyo, seeking Soviet assistance (letter attached).

There he emphasises that "we consist of the Left wing of the national movement in India and stick to the most progressive views on socio-economic problems." The letter reached NKVD (Interior Ministry of the Soviet Union), but the Soviets did not act upon Netaji's request

-10-
'ARZI HUKUMATE AZAD HIND
(INTERIM GOVERNMENT OF FREE INDIA)

[pic 2a]

Imperial Hotel, Tokyo
Monday, 20 November 1944

To

His Excellency,
Soviet Ambassador in Tokyo

Your Excellency,

Being in Tokyo, I would very much want to call on Your Excellency. Having this in mind, I set as my objective mu objective to seek the support of the Soviet Government, through Your Excellency, in India's struggle for its independence.
2.   The fact that we are closely linked with the Axis Powers in the common struggle against Anglo-Americans does not stop me. I am happy to state that the Axis Powers have a clear view about the peculiarities of the problems of India and that they have kindly granted formal recognition to the Interim Government of Azad Hind (Free India), for which we are grateful.   Besides Japan, whose relations with the Soviet Government are of a strictly neutral character, even the German Government has fully understood our stand and fully

>>

>> [pic 2b]

Government has fully understood our stand and fully appreciated the fact that we, Indians, are interested only in actions against Britain and America. The German Government also understood and appreciated the fact that we are not interested in actions against Soviet Russia. In fact, the activities of my organistion in Europe are exclusively against the British and Americans but not against Soviet Russia. This was the basis for our cooperation with the Axis Powers in Europe and in this connection we have complete understanding and approval from the German Government and the Fascist Italian Government.

3.   I am aware of the fact that there exists at present a union between the Soviet Government and the Government of Britain and USA. However, I have a fair knowledge about international politics to understand that this union cannot restrict the Soviet Government in extending support to our struggle for independence. I recall, with great pleasure, the help extended to me by the Soviet Government when I left India in 1941. I conveyed my profound gratitude to the Minister of Foreign Affairs, Mr. Molotov in a letter sent from Berlin, which I hope, would have been duly received by His Excellency.

4.   I am also inspired by the fact that Lenin had always supported the struggle of colonial countries for

>>

>>   [pic 2c]

their independence. As far as I am aware even after the
demise of Lenin, the Soviet Government has not altered
its policy towards the problems of the colonial
countries, including India
5.   Regarding my Party - Forward Bloc- I can say that
at a time, when Soviet foreign policy in Europe was
deplored by all parties in India during 1939-40, we were
the ones, who publicly supported the Soviet foreign
policy towards Germany and Finland.   Moreover,   we
consist of the Left Wing of the national movement in
India and stick to the most progressive views on socio-
economic problems. Besides, on date our party is the
only party in India, which leads an uncompromising
struggle against British Imperialism, in cooperation
with a few other revolutionary groups.
6.   I would very much like to call on Your Excellency
and seek the Soviet Government's assistance through Your
Excellency for our struggle for independence.   As
regards the nature of help which the Soviet Government
may like to render us this should be decided by the
Soviet Government in connection with the prevailing war
situation.   I would only like to add that we are fully
determined to make India completely free and   the
Governments which have recognised the Interim Government
of Free India unconditionally agree with us on this
issue.

     Let me assure , Your Excellency, of my highest
consideration and I await your early reply.
     With regards,
                                    Subhash Chandra Bose

9

Netaji and the Soviet Communists

The "Stupid Fairy Tale"

News of Netaji's death in a plane crash in 1945 was accepted by the USSR (refer NKVD Certificate dated 25.12.45, attached).

Sita Ram Goel, an anti-communist, anti-Islamist, pro-Hindutwa writer; in his book 'Netaji and the CPI' of 1955, at pg. 52, very sensibly quotes Pravda of 7 Jan. 1946, on Netaji's supposed escape to Russia calling it nothing but a "stupid fairy tale" (see attachment).

The Soviet Communists not only took Netaji to be an MI-6 collaborator but used derogatory language against him such as "notorious would be quisling of India," "in Hitlerite pay," "in the pay of Japanese imperialists,' "fascist rogue," etc.

It may be recollected that Netaji's appeal of 20 Nov. '44 to the Soviet Ambassador in Tokyo, asking for Soviet assistance, went to waste.

Yet many believe Netaji trusted the USSR.

The communist campaign against Netaji was rounded off by Moscow in January 1946 as it was started by Moscow in 1930. Writing in *Pravda* dated January 7, 1946 the Soviet journalist David Zaslavsky denounced as " a stupid fairy tale " the report that Subhash Chandra Bose was in Soviet Russia. He wrote : " The substance of the fairy tale is as follows. The notorious would-be quisling of India, Subhash Chandra Bose, who at first was in Hitlerite pay in Berlin and then in the pay of Japanese imperialists in Toyko, has allegedly fled to Russia and has been there since the unconditional surrender of Japan together with his soldiers of the Indian National Army who were taken prisoners by the Russian army. This *fascist rogue* is alleged to have freely travelled in Soviet countries and inspected his 30,000 strong army. But the story does not end here. An unnamed soldier appears to know that responsible representatives of the Soviet Government conferred with Bose and gave this Indo-Fascist adventurer imaginary concrete promises. Such is the stupid fairy tale. In the interests of peace and friend-ship one must nail down newspaper lies. "

-12-

"CERTIFICATE"   **from KGB file**

After the Japanese capitulation in the first half of September 1945, TASS quoting British sources informed from Tokyo that Subhash Chandra Bose, staying in Japan, died.

Deputy Head of IIIrd section of the Vth dept.
Ist Directorate of NKVD of USSR
Lt. Col. Nabatnikov
25.12.1945

For KGB, Bose's case was closed.

10

Muthuramalingam Thevar

Thevar, a colleague of Subhas Bose, Deputy Chairman of Forward Bloc, announced in 1949 that Netaji was alive. But he told different things at different times as evident from his press statements:

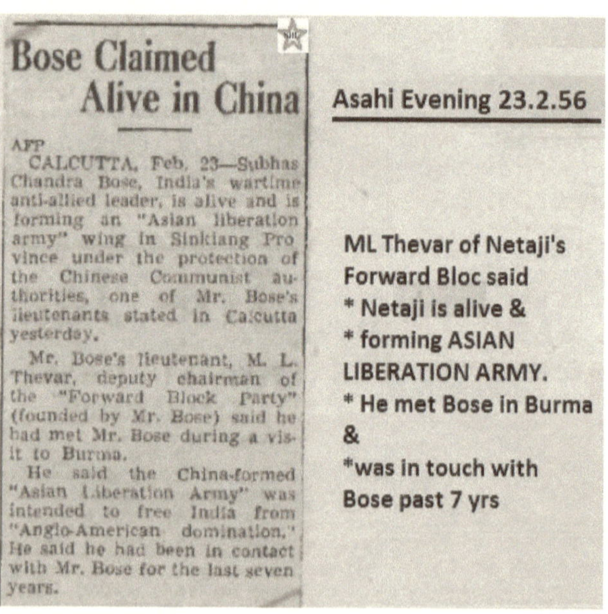

Bose Claimed Alive in China

AFP

CALCUTTA, Feb. 23—Subhas Chandra Bose, India's wartime anti-allied leader, is alive and is forming an "Asian liberation army" wing in Sinkiang Province under the protection of the Chinese Communist authorities, one of Mr. Bose's lieutenants stated in Calcutta yesterday.

Mr. Bose's lieutenant, M. L. Thevar, deputy chairman of the "Forward Block Party" (founded by Mr. Bose) said he had met Mr. Bose during a visit to Burma.

He said the China-formed "Asian Liberation Army" was intended to free India from "Anglo-American domination." He said he had been in contact with Mr. Bose for the last seven years.

Asahi Evening 23.2.56

ML Thevar of Netaji's Forward Bloc said
* Netaji is alive &
* forming ASIAN LIBERATION ARMY.
* He met Bose in Burma &
*was in touch with Bose past 7 yrs

On 23 Feb. '56, he tells Jap newspaper, 'Asahi Evening' that *(image 1)*

1. Bose is alive

2. He met Bose in Burma

3. He was in touch with Netaji for the past 7 yrs.

4. Bose is forming 'Asian Liberation Army' in Sinkiang province next to the Indian border, to liberate India from the Anglo-Americans but on 4 April '56, when he was made to appear before the Shahnawaz Khan Committee, he was not prepared to record anything on Netaji being alive *(image 2).*

Thevar's deposition to SnKhan Comm on 4 April'56 (gist)

Chairman:	You are in touch with Netaji?
Thevar:	Before going into the matter and deposing before the Committee constituted by a Government, I must know the status of that Government towards the man who is considered to be a war criminal.
Shri Bose:	May I take that you are going to make different statements at different places.
Thevar:	It need not be stated here.
Shri Bose:	It is clear that you are unwilling to make any statement.
Thevar:	Without knowing whether he is a war criminal or not.

He dodged cross-examination on the grounds that he belongs to a political party and would not disclose secrets to a Government-appointed Committee. Yet, next month on 12 May '56, he went ahead again to tell 'Nippon Times,' another Jap paper that *(image 3)* he had extensive correspondence with Bose and he is now living in China and is engaged in some mission. He added that Bose would re-emerge when his mission is completed.

Riddle of Chandra Bose

By N. S. ANANTH

Over 10 years after the reported death of Subhas Chandra Bose, the Government of India has set up a commission to go thoroughly into the matter of his death. The commission, composed of two of Bose's close associates and his elder brother has now arrived in Tokyo in the course of its inquiries.

Ever since the end of World War II there have been recurrent rumors in India to the effect that Bose has been seen in various places. He has been reported as having been seen in Indian villages, in China, in Russia and elsewhere. The Government of India has often been asked what proof it has that Bose really died as has been reported.

One question which is often raised is why Bose does not show himself if he is alive. A hero's welcome awaits him if he returns to India. According to some people, he can even pose a challenge to Nehru as a leader. His past career does not belie it. Besides, his wife and daughter are still alive in Europe. These factors seem to show that he is indeed dead.

On the other hand, Muthuramalinga Thevar of South India has stated that he has had extensive correspondence with Bose, who according to him, is now living in China and is engaged in some mission. According to Thevar, Bose will re-emerge when his mission is completed.

For a long time, the Government of India did not display any interest in the matter. They accepted Bose's death as settled and left it at that. Last August the First Secretary of the Indian Embassy in Tokyo attended a memorial service held for Bose in the Renkoji Temple in Tokyo.

Last September, Prime Minister Nehru stated in reply to a question by H. V. Kamath on the floor of the Lok Sabha (Lower House of Indian Parliament) "We cannot simply interfere in their (Japan's) territory, more especially also because all the principal witnesses are either Japanese Government officials or others connected with the Government."

Despite this understandable reluctance, the Indian Government had to bow to the mounting pressure and appoint a commission to inquire into the matter, so great has Bose's stature become.

Bose and his Indian National Army has now grown into legendary proportions in India. The life of this man was such that it could easily pass into legend. The mystery of his reported death was the catalyst which brought it to that stage.

He was born in the holy city of Cuttack on Jan. 23, 1897 to a distinguished family. After a brilliant scholastic career, which was marred by one incident, involving a fight with a British professor on account of the professor's manhandling some Indian students, for which he was suspended from the University for a period of two years, he proceeded to England to study for the Indian Civil Service. After passing the examination, he gave up the Civil Service, the first man to do so, because he felt it repugnant to serve a bureaucracy which held India in bondage. He then re

Nippon Times
12.5.56

Thevar was having extensive correspondence with Bose who was living in China   >>

In actuality, neither was there any 'Asian Liberation Army' in real nor did we see any "mission" that phantom Netaji "was engaged in."

To hog the limelight, Thevar would say anything to the press but would not say anything to the Investigation Committee and skirted cross-examination.

The various conspiracy theorists have been picking up these stray statements of Thevar on numerous occasions in support of their theories. But they perhaps intentionally avoided quoting the President of Forward Bloc Sardar Sardul Singh Caveeshar's announcement as that would put at risk their theories. Caveeshar announced before 19 Dec. '46 that he had learnt "on good authority" that Netaji was shot dead on the Russo-Chinese border by Allied troops (*image 1, Chapter 1*). Caveeshar did not give fodder to the conspiracy theorists.

11

This Is for the Putinists

This is for the information of all doubters of PM Modi to note that Modi had taken up Netaji issue with Russian President Vladimir Putin, during his meeting in Dec. 2015.

Then foreign secretary S. Jaishankar said, "The Netaji issue has figured in our discussion very recently. Let's wait and see what happens." Links to the Foreign Ministry video clip is given below.

An unconfirmed source reported that Modi had got carried away by people preposterously telling him Bose died in Siberia because of Jawaharlal Nehru. It is felt that he should never have brought up the subject with Putin after Russia's clear rebuttals in 1992 and 1995 on Netaji's stay in the Soviet Union in and after 1945. It irritated the Russians. (refer Chapter 2: The Oft-repeated "Russia Has Vital Information") The response Russia gave was nothing but a diplomatic rebuff.

Link to Jaishankar's statement on YouTube is given below:

https://www.youtube.com/attribution_link?a=FWQDII0MO6
Uandu=%2Fwatch%3Fv%3DNvZeHbR3v4s%26feature%3D
shareandfbclid=IwAR3vjPMV7fGCoDno854ftKPyGpqxv_N-
Nw4C9XuCrHky1ZJI0yvJxNEdXsg

https://youtu.be/NvZeHbR3v4s

12

What Happened to 'Tashkent Netaji'?

'A'>'B'>'C'>'D'

A video link is given at the end of this chapter, of an interview taken on 25.5.2015 where it is being said that one of Lal Bahadur Shastri's grandsons told his colleague Chandra Kr Bose that Lal Bahadur told his son Vijay Nath Singh (btw! there was no son of his by that name):

> *"…what to tell you … I have met Subhas Chandra Bose, and I shall bring him along with me. Do not announce anything now … I want to give the people of India a surprise …"*

The story given in the video remained unverified as Lal Bahadur died the same night after signing the 'Tashkent Treaty.'

That was in 1966 while this public announcement is of 2015.

This is another case of 'A' telling 'B' that 'C' said that 'D' saw Netaji. Wonder why the 'D'-s never speak for themselves.

Our immediate concern is not how Shastri died, but our concern is what happened to that 'Netaji' (the Tashkent Man) mentioned by Chandra Bose? Was he bumped off by the Soviet Communists? No one seems to be interested in finding that out, not even his grandson, as there is no political gain in that. Instead of getting a proper investigation done they keep pointing fingers at Congress in Shastri's death.

According to Gumnami baba propagator, his 'Netaji' (the 'Paris Man') could not be in Tashkent at that time, Jan. 1966, as he was recuperating in Faizabad.

https://youtu.be/jcXvnyP1x8k

'Tashkent photos may solve Shastri death mystery'

Prithvijit Mitra| TNN | Dec 14, 2015, 12.09 PM IST

* * * * * * *

Netaji researcher Anuj Dhar believes the files on Shastri could have leads on his mysterious death. But the man in the Tashkent photographs was not Netaji, he said. "This man is lik ely to be a Pakistani diplomat.He might bear resemblances to Netaji but it's not him. There is strong evidence to suggest Netaji was then in Faizabad," said Dhar.

13

The Russian Theory Has Nothing to Stand On: Gumnamists

A book 'Netaji Subhas Chandra Bose: Feared Even in Captivity,' by Santanu Banerjee, published in 2018, propagating the 'Russian theory' invited a panic reaction from the Gumnamists.

A comment on the book, "Purabi Roy also supported Russian point of view" (implying Netaji's physical end in Russia) triggered the following reaction from Gumnami Baba propagator:

- "(Roy) supported with what sir?

- Which file?

- Which eyewitness?

- Who saw Netaji being shot or killed in Russia?

- Which KGB file talks about it?"

- "Sir, there is no proof at all, except for a conspiracy theory that has nothing to stand on. Yet these people are circulating it as if it is gospel truth."

Yes, Mr. Gumnamist, on the same analogy, the assumption that Netaji lived beyond 1945 and entered India, can similarly be questioned:

- "(Baba) supported with what sir?

- Which file?

- Which eyewitness?

- Who saw Netaji entering India?

- Which Indian file talks about it?"

- "Sir, there is no proof at all, except for various conspiracy theories that have nothing to stand on. Yet Gumnamists are misleading people with unestablished stories claiming them as gospel truth."

What is good for the goose is good for the gander.

14

Morarji Desai's View
on Netaji's Death

January 16, 1978

My dear Majumdar,

Thank you for your letter of 13th December 1977, regarding Netaji Subhas Bose. I have had the sixth volume of the printed record of the Transfer of Power 1942-47 looked into but we have not been able to find evidence to sustain the inference that Subhas Bose did not die in the air crash on 18.8.1945. In fact there is a reference to the Japanese announcement that he had died in the air crash. The reference to that matter in the volume is presumably because they were not sure whether the Japanese announcement was correct. In these circumstances, I don't think that this needs any further investigation to establish that he did not die in the aircrash. In fact subsequent inquiries made it quite clear beyond reasonable doubt that he died in the aircrash. This has been confirmed by more than one inquiry. If it is assumed that he were alive, I do not think he would have remained out of India till now. He would have doubtless come here soon after or later at any time during the last so many years. Even under the law if a person is not heard of for seven years, he is presumed to be dead. In the circumstances, I do not think that any useful purpose would be served by having another investigation since all previous investigations and lapse of time should leave no doubt that Shri Subhas Bose is no more. In case you have in mind any other reference in the volume, please let me know and I shall have it looked into.

Yours sincerely,

(Morarji Desai)

Shri R.C. Majumdar,
4, Bipin Pal Road,
P.O. Kalighat,
Calcutta-26

In response to a letter from historian Ramesh Chandra Majumdar following a meeting between the two in 1977 on the issue of Netaji's death, Desai confirmed to Majumdar on 16 Jan. 1978:

"I have had the VIth volume of the printed record of the Transfer of Power 1942–47 looked into, but we have not been able to find evidence to sustain the inference that Subhas Bose did not die in the air crash on 18.8.45."

"I don't think that this needs any further investigation to establish that he did not die in the air crash. In fact, subsequent inquiries made it quite clear beyond any reasonable doubt that he died in the air crash."

"If it is assumed that he was alive, I do not think he would have remained out of India till now. He would have doubtless come here soon after or later at any time during the last so many years."

"Even under the law if a person is not heard of for seven years, he is presumed to be dead."

15

Misinformation Spread
in the Name of Desai

This is for those experts who spread misinformation that Morarji Desai dismissed the Shahnawaz Khan and Justice Khosla Commission Reports.

The fact is just the opposite.

"Evidence being the same it is most unlikely that any new light can be thrown on the matter which might compel the reversal of the earlier findings,"

Desai, in 1978, thus rejected the formation of any new Inquiry Commission.

<u>Desai's observation, Aug '78, on Guha's motion on fresh inquiry</u>

There have been two enquiries into the report of the death of Netaji Subhas Chandra Bose in the air-crash on 18th August 1945 at Taihoku airfield during his air-journey to Manchuria, one by a Committee presided over by Maj. General Shah Nawaz Khan and second by a One-man Committee of Inquiry headed by Shri G.D. Khosla, retired Judge of the Punjab High Court. The majority report of the first Committee and Shri Khosla held the report of death as true. Since then, reasonable doubts have been cast on the correctness of the conclusions reached in the two Reports and various important contradictions in the testimony of witnesses have been noticed. Some further contemporary official documentary records have also become available. In the light of those doubts and contradictions and those records, Government consider that it would be very difficult to regard these findings as conclusive. At the same time Government feels that evidence being the same it is most unlikely that any new light can be thrown on this matter which might compel a reversal of the earlier findings. They, therefore, consider that no useful purpose would be served by having any further inquiry. Government hope that in the light of this statement the Hon. Member will withdraw his Motion.

This portion is reflected in JMCI Report as Desai's response to Samar Guha's motion

This portion is omitted from Samar Guha, Chitta Basu & JMCI quotes

This is a draft approved by PM Desai & shown to Samar Guha

TOP SECRET

No.25/4/NGO(Pt)-Vol.V
Ministry of External Affairs
New Delhi

NOTE FOR THE CABINET

Subject :   Proposal to bring the mortal remains of
Netaji Subhas Chandra Bose from Japan to
India.

d)   Shri Samar Guha moved a Motion in Lok Sabha on August 3, 1977, urging the Government to set up a 3-man commission for conducting a fresh inquiry into the mystery of the disappearance of Netaji. The motion was discussed at length in 1977 and also in 1978. On the 28th August, 1978 the Prime Minister intervening in the debate observed:

"There have been two enquiries into the report of the death of Netaji Subhas Chandra Bose in the air-crash on 18th August, 1945 at Taihoku airfield during his air-journey to Manchuria, one by a Committee presided over by Maj.General Shah Nawaz Khan and the second by a one-man Commission of Inquiry headed by Shri G.D. Khosla, retired Judge of the Punjab High Court. The majority report of the first Committee and Shri Khosla held the report of the death as true. Since then, reasonable doubts have been cast on the correctness of the conclusions reached in the two reports and various important contradictions in the testimony of witnesses have been noticed. Some further contemporary official documentary records have also become available. In the light of those doubts and contradictions and those records Government find it difficult to accept that the earlier conclusions are decisive. At the same time Government feels that no useful purpose would be served by having any further inquiry. I hope that in the light of this statement my Hon. friend will withdraw his motion".

Thereafter Prof. Guha withdrew his motion. While doing so he declared in the House:

VIEWS OF OTHER IMPORTANT MEMBERS OF NETAJI'S FAMILY

13.   While Dr. Sisir Bose supports the idea of bringing back the ashes, Late Amiya Nath Bose, Netaji's nephew had been the most vociferous skeptic of the air crash episode and had opposed any proposal of bringing back the ashes.

14.   This issues with the approval of the External Affairs Minister.

(Salman Haidar)
Foreign Secretary

April'96 Note of the MEA

The 2nd attachment is a Cabinet Note on the issue dated April 1996 where Desai's observation is given as:

"... The Government feels that no useful purpose would be served by having any further inquiry. I hope in the light of the statement my Hon, friend (Samar Guha) will withdraw his motion." Thereafter, Prof. Guha withdrew his motion.

The 1st attachment is the approved draft of the Parliamentary speech by Desai in Aug. 1978, which states: *"Evidence being the same it is most unlikely that any new light can be thrown on the matter which might compel the reversal of the earlier findings."* This draft was shown to Samar Guha before Desai made his speech in the parliament.

The 3rd is the concluding para of Desai's reply dated 2 Feb. 1978, to Guha:

"...any fresh investigation seems to me a sheer waste of money or any other controversy about it a sheer waste of time."

the air crash. The Japanese reported to that effect and the report appears to have been accepted at the tim So many years after the event any fresh investigation seems to me to be a sheer waste of money or any further controversy about it a sheer waste of time. In the circumstances I would advise you to let the matter rest where it is.

With kind regards,

Yours sincerely,

(Morarji Desai)

Prof. Samar Guha, M.P.,
14, Talkatora Road,
New Delhi.

Concluding para of lt. dt. 2 Feb 1978 to Samar Guha

4th is the reply dated 16 Jan. 1978, to RC Majumdar, *"I don't think that this needs any further investigation to establish that he did not die in the air crash."* (This information is given in the previous chapter as well)

January 16, 1978

My dear Majumdar,

Thank you for your letter of 13th December 1977, regarding Netaji Subhas Bose. I have had the sixth volume of the printed record of the Transfer of Power 1942-47 looked into but we have not been able to find evidence to sustain the inference that Subhas Bose did not die in the air crash on 18.8.1945. In fact there is a reference to the Japanese announcement that he had died in the air crash. The reference to that matter in the volume is presumably because they were not sure whether the Japanese announcement was correct. In these circumstances, I don't think that this needs any further investigation to establish that he did not die in the aircrash. In fact subsequent inquiries made it quite clear beyond reasonable doubt that he died in the aircrash. This has been confirmed by more than one inquiry. If it is assumed that he were alive, I do not think he would have remained out of India till now. He would have doubtless come here soon after or later at any time during the last so many years. Even under the law if a person is not heard of for seven years, he is presumed to be dead. In the circumstances, I do not think that any useful purpose would be served by having another investigation since all previous investigations and lapse of time should leave no doubt that Shri Subhas Bose is no more. In case you have in mind any other reference in the volume, please let me know and I shall have it looked into.

Yours sincerely,

(Morarji Desai)

Shri R.C. Majumdar,
4, Bipin Pal Road,
P.O. Kalighat,
Calcutta-26

16

Lal Bahadur Shastri's View on Netaji's Death

Some website and Facebook groups are propagating that PM Lal Bahadur Shastri was in favour of a fresh probe on Netaji's fate and he wanted to know the truth about Netaji. Some persons are blindly, sharing this strange theory without judging authenticity.

The fact is that there is evidence to show that Shastri never doubted death in a plane crash and he refused to conduct a fresh probe.

1. He made this clear in his reply to a Parliament Question in the LS on 23 Nov. 1964.

2. He reiterated his stand while replying to pressmen at Varanasi on 27 Dec. 1964. He added that he would contact Prafulla Sen, CM of WB, to reiterate the position in view of propaganda being carried out in certain quarters.

3. Prafulla Sen contradicted the propaganda in Shastri's presence in Kolkata on 12 Jan. 1965.

4. The position was again made clear in reply to Parliament Question on 2 March 1965.

5. Yet again, the Foreign Minister in response to a Parliament Question reiterated Government's acceptance of the Shah Nawaz Committee findings.

All this despite:

a. Netaji's elder brother Suresh Bose making a statement in Madurai in Feb. 1966 that "Netaji is alive today" and that "he would be back in India in March" (Like many other prophesies this also proved incorrect).

b. Netaji's nephew Dwijendranath Bose also stated at around the same time that "Netaji was still alive and was working at a place very near the borders of India…and would come out into the open and enter India at the appropriate time in such a way that he can establish a new order in the country" (time proved this also to be incorrect).

The attached image of the message by Lal Bahadur Shastry clearly puts forward Shastri's stand:

"… How very sad that just when he was about to see the fulfilment of his life's mission, the cruel hand of death snatched him away from our midst. And yet he lives in our memory and provides an inspiring example."

The Government of India added in the Rajya Sabha on 17 May 1966 in reply to a question that "the Press of India being free we could not prevent people from continuing to make statements about Netaji being alive."

The Government also said, "Government cannot move in this (bringing the ashes) matter unless Netaji's family accepts that Netaji is in fact no longer alive and that these ashes are really his."

PRIME MINISTER'S HOUSE
NEW DELHI-2

January 5, 1965

M E S S A G E

Netaji Subhas Chandra Bose has a unique place in India's political history. Inspired by burning patriotism and an indomitable will, he was, for nearly two and a half decades, among the foremost fighters for the country's freedom. One of the bravest patriots, he staked his all so that India may live. His services to the nation are great as they are glorious and his deeds will be remembered for many generations to come. How very sad that just when he was about to see the fulfilment of his life's mission, the cruel hand of death snatched him away from our midst. And yet he lives in our memory and provides an inspiring example.

(Lal Bahadur)

17

US War Department's View on Netaji's Fate, June 1946

In 1945–46, while investigations by the Allied Forces on the reported death of Netaji were on, the US War Department Memo dated 20 June 1946 read:

> *"There is no direct evidence that Subhas Chandra Bose was killed in an airplane crash in Taihoku, Formosa, despite the public statement of the Japanese to that effect."*

Then, in the following sentence, it says:

> *"Nor is there any evidence available to Intelligence Division, which would indicate that the subject (NSCB) is still alive."*

WAR DEPARTMENT
MILITARY INTELLIGENCE SERVICE
WASHINGTON

ID/CG/WLB
WPL/mos

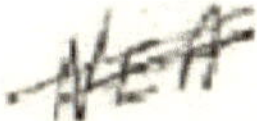

MID 918

30 June 1946

MEMORANDUM FOR: Mr. Jack D. Neal, Chief
Division of Foreign Activity Correlation
Department of State
Washington 25, D. C.

SUBJECT: Subhas Chandra Bose, Request for Information regarding

1.   A search of the files in the Intelligence Division reveals that there is no direct evidence that SUBHAS CHANDRA BOSE was killed in an airplane crash at Taihoko, Formosa, despite the public statement of the Japanese to that effect. Nor is there any evidence available to Intelligence Division which would indicate that the subject is still alive.

2.   Possibly a determination of the facts in this matter could be made by G-2 of the Supreme Commander for the Allied Powers, in Tokyo. It is believed that a request for such information could properly be made through the British representative to the Allied Control Council, Japan.

FOR THE CHIEF, COLLECTION GROUP:

RALPH E. CURTISS
Lieut. Colonel, Inf.
Chief, Washington Liaison Branch.

Extracts from investigation
conducted by the British in
1946 (Figgess Report)

It further goes on to say that *"determination of facts could be made by... Supreme Commander for the Allied Powers, in Tokyo"*

What came out from Tokyo a month later is the Figgess Report, dated 24 July 1946, which read *"It is confirmed as certain that SC Bose died in a Taihoku Military Hospital…on 18th August 1945."*

☆Extracts from investigation conducted by the British in 1946 (Figgess Report)

United Kingdom Liaison Mission,
in Japan,
British Embassy,
Tokyo.

OFFICE OF MILITARY ADVISER.

Report on the Death of Subhas Chandra Bose.

2.   As a result of a series of interrogations of individuals named in the following paragraphs it is confirmed as certain that S.C. Bose died in a TAIHOKU Military Hospital (NAMMON Ward) some time between 1900 hours and 2000 hours local time on the 18th August, 1945. The cause of death was heart failure resulting from multiple burns and shock. All the persons named below were interrogated at different times but the several accounts of the event agree both in substance and detail at all points where the knowledge of the subjects could have been deemed to be based on common experience. The possibility of a pre-arranged fabrication must be excluded since most of the individuals concerned had no opportunity of contact with one another prior to interrogation.

Sgd. J.G. FIGGESS
Lt Colonel.
Tokyo, 25th July 1946.

18

Allied Military Authorities in Tokyo Confirm Netaji's Death, Oct. 1946

The Allied Military Authorities in Tokyo, after careful interrogation of Japanese high-ups, confirmed Netaji's death.

Attached is the newspaper article from 'Free Press Journal,' dated 30.10.1946, reporting on the death of Subhas Chandra Bose.

"JAPANESE CONFIRM NETAJI'S DEATH (FREE PRESS OF INDIA)

Fourteen months ago the Japanese News Agency announced to the world that the plane in which Netaji was flying from Singapore to Tokio had crashed in Formosa. Afflicted India was rudely shaken by this sad news. But she was tantalised all the more by the spate of conflicting reports appearing in the press about his supposed secret flight to Germany to seek haven in Hitler's Reich. Pandit Nehru's recent statement about the death of this Apostle of Indian Freedom provoked a reply from a Forward Blocist. All the way from Singapore, now comes news, from our own Correspondent, that the Allied Military Authorities in Tokio, after careful interrogation of Japanese high-ups have been able to confirm his death."

SINGAPORE. Oct. 29 (By Air Mail)

Details of the investigation, conducted by the Allied Military Authorities in Tokyo, of the plane crash in which Subhas Bose was reported to be killed are now available.

The following press note has been issued:

An in-depth investigation has been conducted in Tokyo, at the request of SACSEA, to establish the precise details of the circumstances surrounding the reported death of Subhas Chandra Bose. The United Kingdom Liaison Mission in Japan conducted these investigations, and it is confirmed as certain that Subhas Chandra Bose died in a Talhoku Military Hospital (Nammon Ward) sometime between 19.00 hours and 20.00 hours, local time, on August 18, 1945. The cause of death was heart failure resulting from multiple burns and shock.

All the persons named below were interrogated at different times, but the several accounts of the event agree both in substance and detail at all points where the knowledge of the subjects could have been deemed to be based on common experience. The possibility of a pre-arranged fabrication must be excluded since most of the individuals concerned had no opportunity of contact with one another prior to interrogation.

FELLOW PASSENGER TELLS TALE

LT.-COL. NONOGAKI: This person was a passenger on the same plane with Bose from Saigon onwards. He related the story of the crash in great detail and drew a sketch showing the position of the crew and passengers. The aircraft was a K.21 Heavy Bomber (Sally). Just after taking off from the Talhoku airstrip en route to Tokyo at about 1430 hours on August 18, 1945, there was a sudden explosion in the port engine, which broke off from the main plane causing the aircraft to go into a spin and crash to the ground, just off the end of the runway. The fuselage burst open, and the petrol tanks exploded on impact with the ground. According to Nonogaki, the following persons were killed instantly:

Three engineers (names unknown).
Wireless Operator (name unknown),
Major Takizawn and
Lt. General Shidel.

The following were very severely burned.
W. O. Noyagi, the pilot,
Major Kono and
Subhas Chandra Bose.

The following were less seriously injured:
Habibur Rahman (personal aide to Bose) and
L-Col. Sakai.

NETAJI SUSTAINS BURNS

Nonogaki gave as the reason for Bose's sustaining such severe injuries that he was sitting next to the petrol tank and owing to the cold had just previously donned a rather tight-fitting type of jacket, which could not easily be removed after the crash when Bose was lying on the ground in flames. Habibur Rahman and Nonogaki between them succeeded in beating out the flames and Bose was removed immediately to a nearby emergency dressing station where the burnt clothing was cut away from his body. He was then taken in a Japanese Army truck in a prostrate condition, but still conscious, to the nearest Army Hospital, known as the Talhoku Military Hospital (Nammon Ward) where he arrived shortly after xx pm.

Lt.-Col. Nonogaki supervised the admittance of Bose to the hospital and heard the report of his subsequent death, but did not himself see any more as he returned to Tokyo by the next departing aircraft.

HE CARRIED BOSE'S ASHES

LT.-COL. SAKAI: Sakai was a passenger sitting immediately behind Nonogaki in the aircraft. He was somewhat shaken by the crash and slightly burned, and so has no clear recollection of what happened immediately after the crash, but for the rest, he confirms the story told by Nonogaki. Sakai was removed to a military hospital but was put in a different ward from Bose and was sufficiently recovered from his injuries to travel to Fukuoka in the same aircraft with Rahman on the 4th/5th September. He carried with him a box alleged to contain the ashes of Bose, but as he was in hospital, he did not himself see Bose again either before or after death.

BODY CREMATED

LT-COL. SHIBUVA MASANORI: This officer was on the staff of Taiwan Army Headquarters, Taihoku. He did not see Bose at any time but was called in to discuss the possibility of transporting Bose's body to Tokyo by plane. After some discussion, this project was dismissed as impracticable, and it was decided to cremate the body. Lt.-Col. Shibuva issued orders for the cremation. He returned to Japan in December after completion of the evacuation of the Japanese surrendered personnel in Formosa.

LT.-COL. TAGAMIVA HIROJI (KEMPEI): This officer, who was also attached to Taiwan Army Headquarters called at the hospital shortly after the crash on the orders of his superior, to enquire about the condition of Bose. He saw Bose who was conscious but obviously in great pain and in a weak state, and on enquiry, he was informed by the doctor present that there was little hope for Bose and that he was sinking fast. He did not see Bose's body after death.

INQUIRY INTO THE ACCIDENT

LT.-COL. MIURA TATSUO: Miura was a staff officer of the 8th Hikishidan attached to the Taiwan Army Air Staff. He did not see Bose at any time either dead or alive but received the first report of the accident from the local airfield company commander (Hikojo Chutai Cho) and was responsible for a subsequent investigation into the cause of the crash. This investigation, by the way, appears to have been very cursory, the explanation offered being that all the staffs in Taihoku were in a turmoil as a result of the sudden ending of the war.

SAT WITH NETAJI ALL NIGHT

SUB.-LT. (MEDICAL) TSURUTA TOYOSHI: At the time of the air accident, Tsuruta held the rank of Probationary Officer and was on duty in the Nammon Ward of the Taihoku Military Hospital. As about 3 o'clock in the afternoon of August 18, he was informed that a V.I.P. suffering from severe injuries had been brought in to the hospital in a truck. Tsuruta supervised the movement of Bose, who was lying on a stretcher without any clothes on and had him taken into the Nananon Ward. Bose was conscious but suffering from terrible third-degree burns on his face and all over his body. The doctor administered a camphor injection and dressed the burns. He says that at the time he recognised that Bose had little chance of surviving. After attending to Bose, Tsuruta dressed the wounds of Habibur Rahman who was burned on the hands and had a superficial head wound. During this time Bose made no conversation except to ask for water, but after he had rested for a little while he asked to talk to Rahman and they carried on a conversation together in an Indian language for some fifteen or twenty minutes. Tsuruta went for his evening meal at about 5:30 p.m. and when he turned to the ward shortly after six o'clock, Bose asked him in English if he would sit with him throughout the night. However, shortly after 7 o'clock p.m. he suffered a relapse, and although the doctor once again administered a camphor injection, he sank into a coma and died shortly afterwards.

DEATH CERTIFICATE

Later, that evening there was a discussion between Tsuruta, Habibur Rahman and another officer, who Tsuruta thinks was probably Lt. Col. Shibuya, as to the possibility of embalming the body and taking it on to Tokyo, but the doctor expressed doubts as to his ability to ensure preservation in the extreme heat. Towards midnight a hastily made coffin arrived from the headquarters of the Taiwan Army and the body was placed in the coffin and covered with a sheet. The following morning the coffin was taken away, and Tsuruta understands that it was cremated although he was not an eyewitness of the process. The death certificate, which was issued by Tsuruta, showed death to be due to heart failure resulting from multiple burns and shock.

When taxed with the question of positive identification of the victim of the accident, Tsuruta stated that there was, of course, no documentary evidence since all the clothes and personal papers were destroyed. It is a matter of common knowledge that Bose was in the aircraft and that there could not possibly be any error in identity.

Tsuruta produced papers to show that he qualified as a medical practitioner from Kyoto Imperial University in September 1943, specialising in surgery.

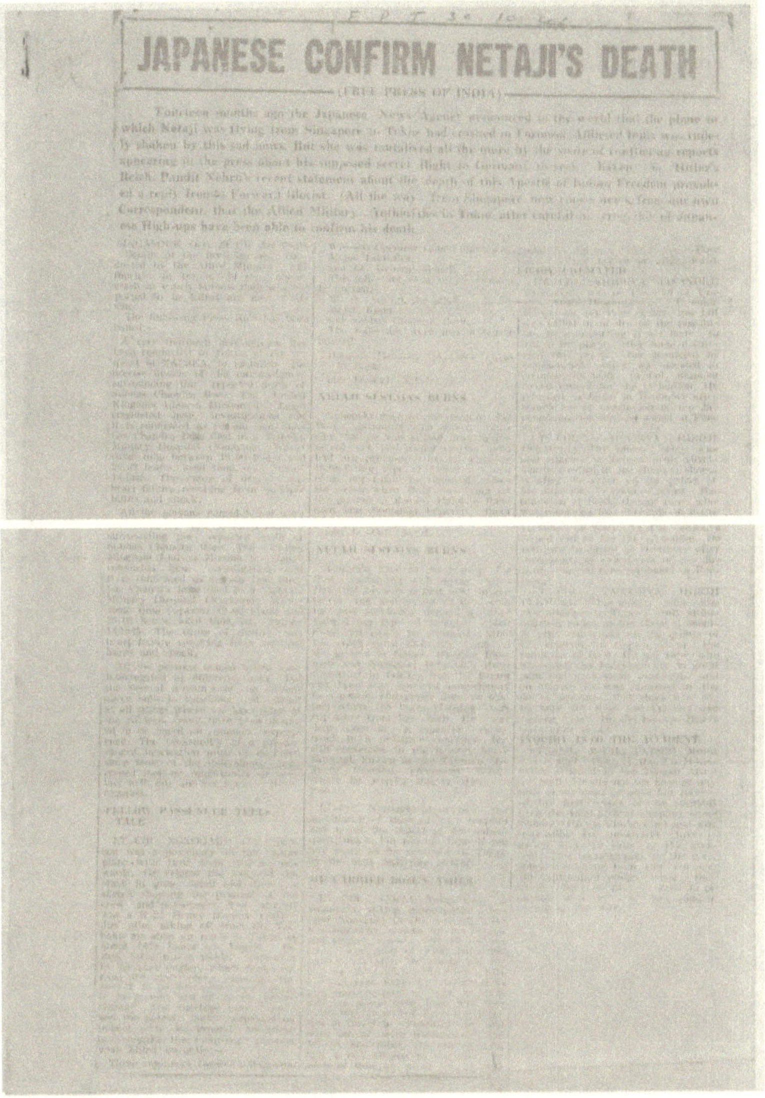

JAPANESE CONFIRM NETAJI'S DEATH

(FREE PRESS OF INDIA)

Fourteen months ago the Japanese News Agency announced to the world that the plane in which Netaji was flying from Singapore to Tokio had crashed in Formosa. Affected India was [deeply] shaken by this sad news. But she was comforted all the more by the story of conflicting reports appearing in the press about his supposed secret flight to Germany to meet ... Hitler's Reich. Pandit Nehru's recent statement about the death of this Apostle of Indian Freedom provoked a reply from Forward Blocist. (All the way) from Singapore now comes our own Correspondent, that the Allied Military Authorities in Tokio after capture ... of Japanese High-ups have been able to confirm his death.

[illegible]

NETAJI SUSTAINS BURNS

[illegible]

TELLING PASSENGER TELL-TALE

[illegible]

NETAJI SUSTAINS BURNS

[illegible]

MENTIONED BOSE'S NAME

[illegible]

INDIA IS TO THE FOREST

[illegible]

SAT WITH NETAJI ALL NIGHT

SUB-LT. (MEDICAL) TSURUTA TOYOSHI: At the time of the uprising, Tsuruta held the rank of Probationary Officer and was on duty in the Nammon Ward of the Taihoku Military Hospital. At about 3 o'clock in the afternoon of August 18, he was informed that a V.I.P. suffering from severe injuries had been brought in to the hospital in a truck. Tsuruta supervised the removal of Bose who was lying on a stretcher without any clothes on and had him taken into the Nammon Ward. Bose was conscious but suffering from terrible third degree burns on the face and all over his body. The doctor administered a camphor injection and dressed the burns. He says that at the time he examined him, Bose had small chance of surviving. After attending to Bose, Tsuruta dressed the wounds of Habibur Rahman who was burned on the hands and had a superficial head wound. During this time Bose made no conversation except to ask for water, but after he had rested for a little while he asked to talk to Rahman and they carried on a conversation together in an Indian language for some fifteen or twenty minutes. Tsuruta went for his evening meal at about 7 p.m., and when he returned to the ward about six o'clock, Bose asked him in English if he would sit with him throughout the night. However, shortly after 7 o'clock p.m. he suffered a relapse and although the doctor once again administered a camphor injection he sank into coma and died shortly afterwards.

DEATH CERTIFICATE

Later that evening there was a discussion between Tsuruta, Habibur Rahman and another officer who Tsuruta thinks was probably Lt.-Col. Shibusa, as to the possibility of embalming the body and taking it by air to Tokyo, but the doctor expressed doubt as to his ability to ensure preservation in the extreme heat. Tsuruta obtained a highly inflammable solution from the headquarters of the Taiwan Army and the body was placed in the coffin and covered with a sheet. The following morning the coffin was taken away and Tsuruta understands that it was cremated, although he was not an eye-witness of the process. The death certificate which was issued in Taihoku showed death to be due to heart failure resulting from multiple burns and shock.

When faced with the question of positive identification of the remains of the accident, Tsuruta stated that there was of course no documentary evidence since all the clothes and personal papers were lost, but it was of common knowledge that Bose was in the aircraft and that there could not possibly be any error in identity.

Tsuruta produced papers to show that he qualified as a medical officer from Kyushu Imperial University in September 1943, specializing in surgery.

19

A Page from CIA File, Sept. 1948

The attached page dated 10 Sept. 1948 from a CIA file clearly shows that Netaji's death was taken for granted by the CIA.

Despite all this documentary evidence, mystery mongers and Netaji traders keep saying that the CIA did not believe in Netaji's death in an air crash.

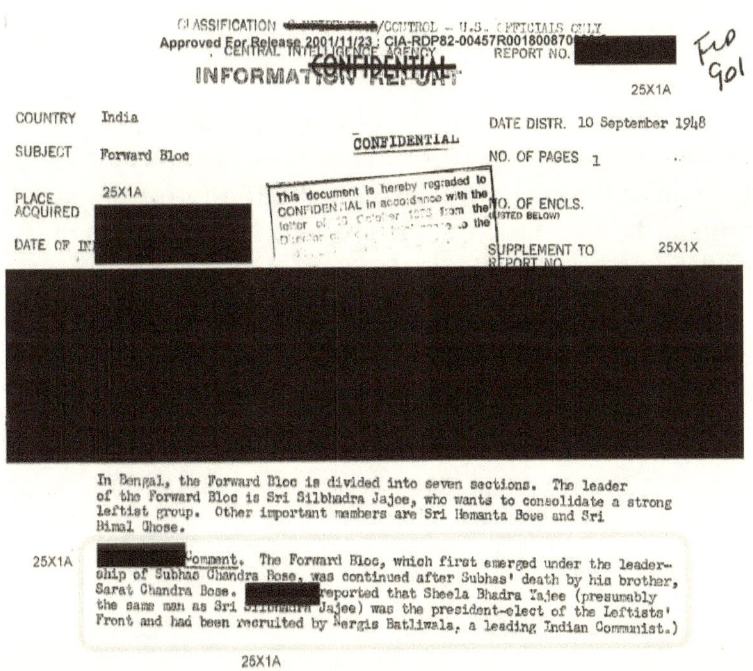

20

CIA: Bose Died in an Airplane Crash in Indochina in the Fall of 1945

Conspiracy theorists often remark that the CIA did not believe in Netaji's death.

Therefore, it is necessary to tell the readers that the said propaganda is absolutely false.

Attached here is a page from the CIA papers released in Aug. 2000. On the subject 'The Left, the Indian Communist and Sarat Ch Bose,' under the sub-head 'Other radical Leftist Parties,' it is clearly mentioned, "Bose died in an airplane crash in Indochina in the fall of 1945…" (underlined in the attachment).

The declassified CIA files can be accessed through the net.

<u>Other radical leftist parties</u>

Between the Socialist Party and the Communist Party are a number of small radical leftist splinter parties, most of which are located in West Bengal. Virtually all of these parties combine some elements of communist or socialist ideology with a virulent nationalism.

Bengal's political history reveals a paradoxical combination of conservatism, docility, and adaptability with a strong and respected tradition of radical idealism, anarchism, and revolution. Bengal's nationalist anarchist movement of the late nineteenth and early twentieth centuries was the forerunner and inspiration of the radical Forward Bloc movement which developed within the Congress Party under the leadership of Subhas Chandra Bose in the late 1930's. The Forward Bloc's advocacy of the use of violence in the struggle for independence constituted a direct challenge to the Gandhian principles then being followed by the party and resulted in the ejection of Bose and his supporters. During World War II Bose, who escaped to Germany and then proceeded to Japan, helped organize Indian soldiers captured by the Japanese in China, Malaya, and Burma, together with a number of Indians in Southeast Asia, into an Indian National Army (INA) with the objectives of winning Indian independence with Japanese military support. Bose died in an airplane crash in Indochina in the fall of 1945 but the British brought a number of the INA officers to trial. This move was generally unpopular in India and particularly in Bengal where Bose was regarded as a hero. As a result most of the defendants were simply denied the right to return to the regular Indian Army and a number of them subsequently became active among left wing splinter groups, particularly in Bengal.

In addition to a revolutionary and extreme nationalist tradition, India's radical left wing groups exhibit to a marked degree the same tendency towards political splintering which is increasingly becoming a characteristic of general Indian political organization. Personal rivalries and conflicts over ideological differences -- often over relatively minor points -- have caused a successive splitting of the left, resulting in the formation of a multitude of groups, none of them individually very strong.

Since independence various leftist leaders have att...

21

Netaji Died in 1945 Air Crash, CIA Documents Say

'One India' published an article of 28 Jan. 2017 reporting that among the 9.3 lac declassified CIA documents posted online, there is a report called 'Forward Bloc,' dated 10 Sept. 1948, which records Bose's demise.

Another Report titled 'India's Communist Parties and organisations' provides details regarding Bose's death in Indochina in the fall of 1945.

The report also quotes 1956 Investigation by the Japanese Government concluding Bose died of injuries sustained in the air crash on Aug. 18, 1945.

The link to the article is given below:

https://www.oneindia.com/india/netaji-died-in-1945-air-crash-declassified-cia-documents-reveal-2330358.html?fbclid=IwAR1HGLtyJEnidMMc7tstqPqCjC7ORn3aQuqC46nu6oVmP5_TExTucMxohg

Netaji died in 1945 air crash, declassified CIA documents reveal

By Vicky | Published: Saturday, January 28, 2017, 11:29 [IST]

Although a class of Indians continues to believe that Subhas Chandra Bose lived past the 1940s a Central Intelligence Agency report, dated 1948, believed he had died in a plane crash in 1945.

Part of some 9.3 lakh declassified documents, running into more than 12 million pages, posted online by the CIA is a report called 'Forward Bloc' dated September 10, 1948, deals with Bose and the conditions of his alleged demise.

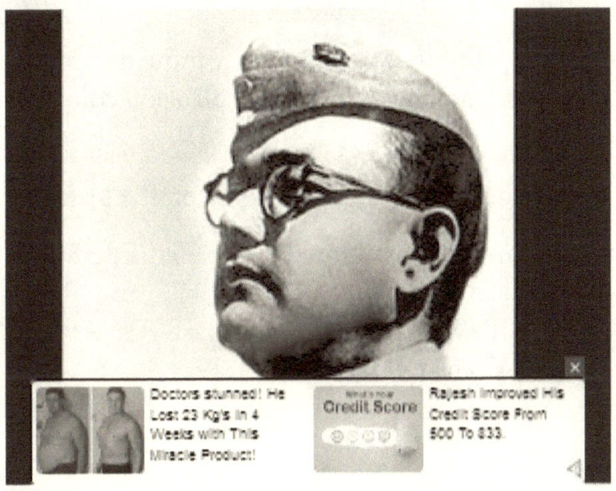

Another report titled 'India's Communist parties and organisations and their influence on workers and trade unions' also provides details regarding Bose's death. The report speaks about his escape from India to Germany during World War II and adds that the fiery freedom-fighter passed away in a plane crash in Indochina in the fall of 1945.

The report also quotes a 1956

22

The Flight Path of Netaji
from CIA Records

The flight path of Subhas Ch Bose on 16, 17 and 18 August 1945.

Completed paths are shown in blue, those not completed due to the plane crash, are shown in red (available in colour in the link given below).

There is no ambiguity in CIA records on the plane crash.

https://commons.m.wikimedia.org/wiki/File:Flight_paths_of_Subhas_Chandra_Bose_on_16,_17,_and_18_August_1945.jpg?fbclid=IwAR34tsGYYEqLJURL_A91_41LO5u AvbqrV7Sitp4LWBm08X4ItasPKvDM3Bs

File:Flight paths of Subhas Chandra Bose on 16, 17, and 18 August 1945.jpg

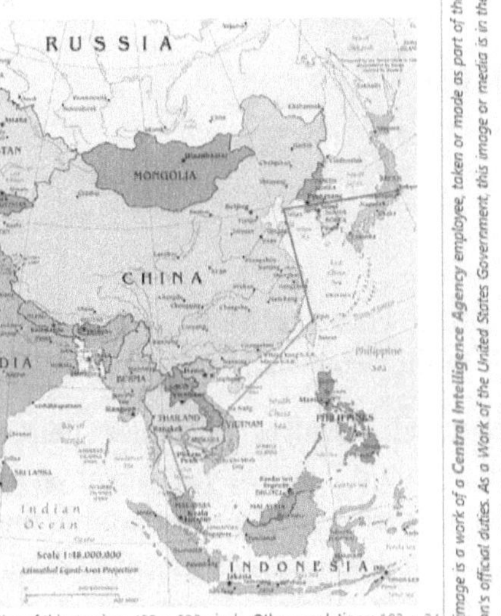

Size of this preview: 455 × 600 pixels. Other resolutions: 182 × 24 × 480 pixels | 583 × 768 pixels | 1,102 × 1,452 pixels.

Original file (1,102 × 1,452 pixels, file size: 679 KB, MIME type: image/jpeg)

This image is a work of a Central Intelligence Agency employee, taken or made as part of that person's official duties. As a Work of the United States Government, this image or media is in the public domain in the United States.

23

French Files

A French historian, Jean-Baptiste Prashant Morè (JBP Morè), claimed that Netaji did not die in the plane crash on 18 Aug. 1945.

He says the French National Archives authority denied him access to a secret file that could have solved the mystery surrounding Netaji's death. He neither names the file no. nor the title of the file. He just says that the French Government had said that the file had been closed for 100 years. He has been, at regular intervals, raising the same issue.

Morè was born to a Marathi, Panjab Rao Morè and Ellenamma Prouchandy, in Pondicherry. His grandfather had played a martyr's role in India's freedom movement due to his association with Netaji Subhash Chandra Bose's struggle for India's independence, in Saigon, says his public profile.

Morè shifted to France after obtaining his bachelor's degree in Pondicherry. After facing several setbacks in his scholarly pursuit, he took to writing 'history.'

One interesting point is that his "theory" neither supports the 'Russian angle' nor the 'Gumnami Baba angle.' His conviction is that Bose's life ended in Saigon sometime in September 1945.

The link for direct access to the DNA India article is given below:

https://www.dnaindia.com/india/report-secret-file-that-could-unravel-mystery-of-netaji-subhas-chandra-bose-s-death-closed-for-100-years-report-2563700?fbclid=IwAR3FkCmmpLDLDfuFUdjufNp9zqF3JtqhubalPRmPI57FQ6XGEnaYOL4CZDY.

Now, a noted French historian has claimed that the a secret file that could have solved the mystery has been 'closed for 100 years'.

According to a Times of India report, historian JBP More tried to access the said file at the French National Archives. However, the authorities denied him the access and said that the file has been 'closed for 100 years'.

'The letter of the French authorities not to allow me to consult a lone file pertaining to the INA and Bose in Saigon has come as a great surprise to me. This goes to affirm my conviction that Bose's life ended in Saigon sometime in September 1945. That is why this file has been classified as out of reach for consultation for 100 years,' More was quoted as saying by the Times of India.

24

Contradiction within 'French Document' and with Russian Theory

On a TV programme on 'Times Now' (1st link given below) on 18th August '17 evening, we heard from the panellist, Chandra Kr Bose, Anuj Dhar and Adheer Som, that as per some (unidentified) French "secret document" Subhas Bose was attending a conference in Hanoi in Nov. '45? … (a)

In the article "Document shows Bose fled from Vietnam prison," published in 'The Hindu' (2nd link) of 2nd Sept. '17, instead, we hear from J.B. Prashanth Morè quoting, also, a French "secret document" that 'Bose was in Vietnam prison' in Saigon that time (Sept.–Dec. '45)! … (b)

When we place the above (a) and (b) face to face, we see that:

- Bose-Dhar-Som telling us Subhas Bose was "attending a conference in Hanoi in Nov. '45."

- JBP Morè informing us that 'Bose was in Vietnam prison' in Saigon during Sept.–Dec. '45!

Thus, with no checking of the claims, both the electronic media and print media are taking observers and readers for a ride in their domain of unreality.

Purabi Roy failed to establish her 'Russian theory' to the Justice Mukherjee Commission of 1999–2005.

Samar Guha's claim when compared to Bose-Dhar-Som's claim and that of JBP Morè's, contradict each other. While between the

104

latter two, one claims Bose was attending a conference in Hanoi in Nov. '45, and the other puts Bose in Saigon prison during Sept.–Dec. '45, Guha claims in his letter to Gorbachov in Nov. '88":

"Subhas Ch Bose arrived at Dairen at 1.30 afternoon on Aug. 23 1945. Bose got into a jeep and proceeded towards Russian territory…"

'The Interpol…published a report in India that Subhas Bose went to Russia after the fall of Japan.'

The funny part is that the conspiracy theorists in over past seven decades could not agree upon Bose's supposed whereabouts post 18 August 1945 with each one of them busy in one-upmanship.

1. https://www.facebook.com/sumeruroychaudhury/videos/10207576136841077/?t=10

2. https://www.thehindu.com/news/national/document-shows-netaji-fled-from-vietnam-prison-says-historian/article19612251.ece

THE HINDU
NATIONAL

Document shows Netaji fled from Vietnam prison, says historian

PUDUCHERRY, SEPTEMBER 02, 2017 23:37 IST
UPDATED: SEPTEMBER 02, 2017 23:37 IST

25

From The British Library:
Sarat Bose and Vietnam

After the exit of Netaji Subhas, while the fate of India's independence cum partition was under consideration and long before the Indian communists raised the slogan আমার নাম তোমার নাম, ভিয়েতনাম! ভিয়েতনাম! (amar naam tomar naam, Vietnam! Vietnam!), Sarat Bose turned his attention towards Vietnam to rid Asia of colonialism.

He appealed to Indian youths to come forward in tens of thousands and raise a volunteer army to fight alongside Vietnam freedom forces.

Attached is a reproduction of an Indian newspaper report dated 4 Jan. 1947, found in the British Library under the section 'Indian Independence': World War 2 and the end of colonialism.

Sarat Chandra Bose's appeal to raise this army and his contacts with Vietnam freedom fighters must have confused some 'researchers' and given rise to the mystery stories of Netaji's post '45 'Asian Liberation Army,' the 'Vietnam War' angle, 'French files,' etc. as both Subhas and Sarat were 'Chandra Bose'-s in the records of both the Japs and the Allies.

HELP FOR RESEARCHERS

 Indian Independence: World War II Source 6

Cutting from Indian Newspaper, *National Call*, 4 Jan 1947
[L/P&S/12/4705]

Sarat Bose Calls for A Volunteer Army To Fight Alongside The Vietnamese

Calcutta, Jan. 3-Maintaining that the future of Asia, including that of India is now being decided on the battlefields of Viet-nam. Mr Sarat Chandra Bose, today appealed to Indian youths to come forward in thousands and tens of thousands to help the Vietnam Republic and to take a volunteer army to fight alongside the Viet-nam republic forces.

He said: The battle of Indo-China is now entering its crucial phase. The French Imperialists are mobilising their entire military and air strength to crush and destroy the young Indo-Chinese Republic and re-establish their colonial mastery over the Indo-Chinese people. It is perhaps not an accident that a squadron of German Junkers transport aircraft is feeding the French Army at Hanoi from Saigon and dive-bombing British Spitfires are clearing the way for French troops advancing on Hanoi. The Western Imperialist Powers are pooling all their resources to smash the liberation movement in one of the ancient historic countries of the East.

"The battle in Indo-China is not merely a war for the freedom of the Indo-Chinese people - It is part, and an essential part, of the larger struggle for Asiatic freedom. The defeat of the Indo-Chinese Republic at the hands of the French Imperialists will mean consolidation and strengthening of Western Imperialism in Asia. It is in Indo-China, therefore, that the battle for Asiatic freedom must be fought and won by the Asiatic peoples. The defeat of French Imperialism in Indo-China will mean the liberation of an important strategic centre in Asia from the stranglehold of Western Imperialism. It is in this context that we should view and analyse the fateful struggle now going on in Indo-China.

We must realize that the fate of India is, to some extent, linked up with the fate of Indo-China. Indian freedom can only be conceived in the background of Asiatic freedom. The complete, and utter distruction of Western Imperialism in Asia is the only guarantee of our future security. We cannot but therefore, take an active interest in the heroic battle that is now being fought by the Indo-Chinese people for their country's freedom. It is not enough for us to express sympathy and pass pious resolutions. Asia's future, including that of India, is now being decided on the battlefields of Viet-Nam. It is time, therefore, that Indian young men should play their part and shed their blood in common with the youth of Indo-China for building the structure of Asiatic freedom. I hope young men from all over the country will come forward in thousands and tens of thousands and volunteer their services to the Viet-Nam Republic. I am aware that the Government of India as at present constituted, may not find it possible to render armed assistance to the Indo-Chinese Republic. But, I believe, there is nothing to prevent an Indian volunteer army from taking their stand along-side the Viet-Nam Republic forces and fighting shoulder to shoulder with them for the common battle of Asia." -API.

26

Sarat Gave Compensation to His Brothers

Sarat Bose gave compensation to his brothers who were occupants and/or shareholders of the Elgin Road house in Kolkata. Sarat's purpose was to convert the building into a memorial for Subhas. This was in the late 1940s. It came to be called Netaji Bhavan. This is where Subhas had mostly lived and worked.

Would Sarat have done what he did if he believed Subhas was still alive?

27

Misinformation

Another misinformation doing the rounds is that: "Sarat Chandra Bose doubted Habibur Rahman on Netaji's death."

Truth: Sarat Chandra Bose did not doubt Habibur Rahman.

Amiya Bose is recorded to have said, "Sarat Chandra Bose did not doubt Habibur Rahman's story."

He went further, stating:

"I remember in December 1945 father took Netaji's death for granted. He was very moved by seeing the watch and said 'same watch…same watch.'"

The above fact is recorded in Justice Khosla's Commission Report, para 4.105 (attached)

This fact and those mentioned earlier have been available with us for years. No one bothers to study them. Most take the easy path of believing hearsays. And the conspiracy theorists make the best out of this sort of ignorance.

Shri Amiya Nath Bose was questioned, in great detail and at considerable length, about this watch. He was inclined to believe the story attributed to Habibur Rahman and to accept the fact that the watch did, in fact, belong to Subhas Chandra Bose. He expressed the opinion that his father Sarat Chandra Bose also did not doubt Habibur Rehman's story. While describing the incident when Mr. Nehru handed the watch to Sarat Chandra Bose, he said :

> "I remember in December 1945 father took Netaji's death for granted. He was very moved by seeing the watch and said 'same watch.........same watch'."

A suggestion was made to the witness that his uncle used to wear a round watch, he said :

> "One thing I heard from many persons is that the round gold watch that he used to wear certainly did not reach Europe.......That particular round gold watch could never come to East Asia."

He reiterated his belief that the round watch, which his uncle used to wear in India, never reached Europe and he had no reason to disbelieve Habibur Rahman's story. He also mentioned a round watch which had been brought by Major Swami and was handed over to Sarat Chandra Bose. This watch too was said to have been worn by Subhas Chandra Bose.

£ 106 Witnesses have made totally contradictory

28

The Supposed Radio Broadcast by Netaji, Post Aug. '45

The conspiracy theorists often mention of some supposed radio broadcast by Netaji after Aug. 1945, in an attempt to prove that he did not die in the plane crash.

So, let us have a look at what they refer to:

(1) SM Goswami, a top-level bureaucrat.

Goswami deposed before Justice Khosla Commn during 1970–74, a story given to him by a friend (see attached 1st 2 pages) that Netaji made 3 broadcasts post Aug. '45. The dates given by him are:

19 Dec. 1945

18 Jan. 1946 and

19 Feb. 1946

Goswami submitted typed scripts of the supposed speeches given to him by his friend, whereabouts of whom he doesn't know.

It may be noted that the supposed broadcast was neither heard by him nor by his friend who gave him the typed script.

(2) Chitta Basu, Forward Bloc MP.

Basu submitted an aide-memoire to PM Narsimha Rao, 20 years later on 11.2.1992, in which, among other issues, he claimed that an official of the Bengal Governor's House, PC Kar, claimed that they picked up 3 broadcasts (see attached last 4 pages) of Netaji on:

26 Dec. 1945

1 Jan. 1946 and

(undated) Feb. 1946

Basu too, like Goswami, didn't hear the broadcast himself. Nor does he mention anyone (then living) to have heard the broadcast. He too, submitted typed scripts.

Now, if one goes through the script, one would notice that the British Prime Minister is mentioned as "Prime Minister of England" by 'Netaji.' Would Netaji be making such a blunder? Doesn't the script remind us of Shyam Lal Jain and his forged letter in the name of Nehru addressed to Attlee?

Also compare Goswami and Basu's claim: their dates of broadcast do not match.

To top it all, there is no record in any contemporary newspaper (Dec. '45 to Feb. '46) of any such broadcast by Netaji.

This is yet another example of how people like SM Goswami and Chitta Basu added fuel to the conspiracy theories, and these are still being used by unscrupulous persons.

Para 6.48 of Khosla Commn Report

The story of the broadcast by Netaji is described in the following manner:

Goswami: Netaji made three broadcasts. First one was on 19th December, 1945, just after one month.
Commission: Did you listen to this broadcast?
Goswami: No, Sir. It was recorded in B.B.C. and one of my friends, a Bengali gentleman, who was working there, was an officer - he practically told that.
Commission: Have you listened to the playing of the tape?
Goswami: No, it was recorded in B.B.C.
Commission: Do you know what the speech was about?
Goswami: Yes, shall I read it out?
Commission: Did you hear the tape being played?
Goswami: How can I?
Commission: Where did you get this note?
Goswami: It was recorded in B.B.C. London.
Commission: Your Bengali friend had given this story to you?
Goswami: Yes.
Commission: What is the name of this Bengali friend?
Shri Goswami: I hesitate to give the name. He has already lost his service when this broadcast was published in a Bengali paper BHARATBARSA

>>

Para 6.48 of Khosla Commn Report

Commission: We want to know how far this broadcast is the true broadcast of Netaji. You did not hear it. You have said that you have not heard it yourself. Unless you give the name of your Bengali friend we can not accept this evidence.

Goswami: Sir, the language is sufficient to give proof.

Commission: We cannot accept that. We must have a person who has heard the broadcast himself. Otherwise this evidence is of no value.

Goswami: Frankly speaking, when I showed this broadcast to Radhakrishnan, he told me, well Goswami, I have heard another broadcast, I said, how is it?

Commission: But you did not hear it. You said three broadcasts. What are the others?

Goswami: The other one was on 18th January, 1946 and the third one was on 19th February, 1946 and this is the fateful broadcast that upset the whole thing. Netaji's one mistake of putting one sentence absolutely shocked the British nation.

Commission: The Bengali friend gave you the typed scripts of all the three broadcasts?

Goswami: Yes.

Commission: You can give them to us. We will try to get copies and ask this Bengali friend to come and give evidence.

Goswami: I do not know where he is now.

Commission: So, you cannot help us to trace him.

Goswami: How can I go on chasing a man who may be either in Japan or London or in Switzerland?

Commission: When did he give you copies of the broadcasts?

Goswami: This broadcast, that gentleman of the B.B.C. came on a trip here. He gave the typed copies to his sister who retained it. Then from the sister some gentleman whose name, with your lordship's permission, I should not say because he is in another service and when he gave it to me and after it was published in BHARATBARSA, Magh, 1387 B. S. he lost his job. BHARATBARSA is a monthly magazine."

Chitta Basu :part of aide-memoire on Radio broadcast

NETAJI SUBHAS CHANDRA BOSE'S BROADCAST AFTER THE ALLEGED AIR CRASH

1. NETAJI'S MESSAGE :   DECEMBER 26 , 1945

" I am at present under the shelter of a great World Powers.
My heart is burning for India .... I will go to India on
the crest of a Third World War. The Third World War is coming soon. It
may come in ten years, or even earlier .... I will sit in
judgement upon those who are trying my men at Red Fort."

Chitta Basu :part of aide-memoire on Radio broadcast

2. NETAJI'S MESSAGE :   JANUARY 1, 1946

" I am giving a very short speech about the Indian National
week to India for my brothers and sisters in India.

We must get freedom within two years. The British Imperialism
is broken down and it must concede independence to India. India will
not be free by means of "Non-violence". But I am quite respectful to
Mr. M. K. Gandhi.

The battle of freedom is not easy. But I can assure you that
we will get freedom of India very soon. I know that many Indians are
waiting for me. I am quite sure to be successful within two years.

I have been informed against the news of the police firing at
Calcutta. Many students are dead. My eyes were full of tears when I
heard it. I know that man is mortal and the most glorious death is
one when a person dies to save his own country. The Indians who shed
their blood for freedom could not die.

My first order to my revolutionary friends in India is that
they will hold a great meeting to commemorate the martyrs on the 25th
inst".

-2-

3. <u>NETAJI'S MESSAGE :</u>   FEBRUARY, 1946

" THIS IS SUBHAS CHANDRA BOSE SPEAKING, JAI HIND. IT IS FOR THE THIRD TIME I AM ADDRESSING MY INDIAN BROTHERS AND SISTERS AFTER JAPAN'S SURRENDER.

THE PRIME MINISTER OF ENGLAND IS GOING TO SEND MR. PETHICK LAWRENCE AND TWO OTHER MINISTERS FROM LONDON WITH NO OBJECT IN VIEW OTHER THAN LET THE BRITISH IMPERIALISM A PERMANENT SETTLEMENT FOR ALL MEANS TO SUCK THE TOTAL BLOOD OF INDIA. NOW, AMONG THESE THREE LONDONERS, ONE HAD TO GO BACK FROM INDIA WITH A BAFFLED HEART ONLY A FEW YEARS AGO.

IT IS AS A SORT OF PRECAUTION, I AM ADVISING INDIANS NOT TO PAY ANY HEED TO THESE IMPOSTERS. I AM SURE THAT MR. PETHICK LAWRENCE WILL HAVE TO SUBMIT AN ADEQUATE EXPLANATION FOR ALL THE MISHAPS AND DISASTERS OF INDIA BY THIS TIME. THE UNDERLYING INTENTION OF THIS ENDEAVOUR BY THE THREE IS NOTHING BUT TO SET A NEW TRAP OF DEPENDENCE IN WHICH INDIA MAY FALL VERY SOON. SO MY EARNEST APPEAL TO THE INDIANS IS THAT THEY SHOULD IN NO CASE HEAR THEM BUT CONTINUE REVOLUTION AGAINST WHAT IS CONTRARY TO ACHIEVE

HEAR THEM BUT CONTINUE REVOLUTION AGAINST WHAT IS CONTRARY TO ACHIEVE FREEDOM. I THINK MANY OTHER VICEROYS AND MINISTERS WILL EMBARK ON INDIA WITH THE SAME MOTTO FOR KEEPING US IN THE DARK DAWN OF DEPENDENCE. BUT MY INDIANS SHOULD NEVER HEAR THEM.

AGAIN I AM ANNOUNCING THAT WITHIN A SHORT PERIOD OF TWO YEARS INDIA WILL HAVE THE DAWN OF INDEPENDENCE. WE WILL HAVE COMPLETE FREEDOM BY THAT TIME AND I WILL ALSO COME BACK IN THE YEAR 1947.

MANY OF THE INDIANS HAVE DECLARED ME AS THE 'NETAJI' OF INDIA BUT I AM TELLING THEM THAT I AM NOTHING BUT AN HUMBLE SON LIKE OTHERS OF 'BHARAT MATA' AND AM NOT ALL WORTHY OF BEING THE SAME.

THE BRITISH IMPERIALISM WILL HAVE ITS UTTER DESTRUCTION AND IT IS NOW COMMENCED. YOU SEE THEY HAVE COME DOWN TO UTTER SHAME BY KILLING OUR CHILDREN ONLY FOR HAVING THEIR IMPERIALISM STILL ABOVE.

29

Another Myth That
You Must Get Rid Of

In opposition to the common belief that Japan agreed to help Netaji to take shelter in Russia, the fact is that the Japanese Government refused to give any support to Netaji to go to Russia. Instead, they said they would drop him in India (see attachments). They were then at war with the Soviets.

The attachment is the English translation of the Telegram received by Netaji from Tokyo through the Southern Command in reply to Netaji's enquiry on the attitude of the Japanese Government to extend facilities to proceed to Russia with some of his associates in the event of Japan's collapse. (The English version is rendered by some Japanese officer as was usual and was submitted along with the original Japanese letter. The Telegram with translation was delivered to Netaji in the 2nd week of June 1945)

Earlier, on 20 Nov. 1944, Netaji wrote to the Soviet Ambassador Y Malik in Tokyo, for Soviet assistance for our struggle for independence. In this letter, he praised Lenin and the Soviet system and reiterated that "we consist of the Left wing of the national movement in India and stick to the most progressive views on socio-economic problems" (see Chapter 8). This letter (translated) was passed on to NKVD on 3 Jan. 1945. The appeal remained ineffective.

COPY OF TOKYO'S TELEGRAM TO SOUTHERN COMMAND REGARDING YOUR EXCELLENCY'S
OPINION FOR THEIR CONSIDERATION.

. . . . . .

1.   The opinion of the Nippon Government with regard to
Your Excellency's plan of approaching the Soviet is as follows:-

(a) Not only the assistance by Nippon Government to Your
Excellency who are firmly determined to co-operate to the last with Nippon
in order to attain the object of Indian Independence remains wholly
unchanged but it also desire to still further strengthen the spiritual tie.

(b) Nippon Government pays a deep respect with its whole heart
to Your Excellency's co-operation with Nippon on the moral strength to the
utmost in order to attain Indian Independence, convinced of Nippon's certain
victory and without resorting in the least to the opportunism of following
in the wake of the powerful in spite of the present unfavourable world
situation to Nippon. It may be added that the reason why the above (a) item
which is apparently needless to mention has been repeated here is that the

[pic 3a]   >> 2

>> 2

[pic 3b]

situation to Nippon. It may be added that the reason why the above (a) item
which is apparently needless to mention has been repeated here is that the
Government more than ever earnestly hopes that Your Excellency will push on
fighting for the liberation of India with firm determination to display the
spirit of live or die together by India and Nippon.

(c) Nippon Government deems it almost without hope of success to
get directly in touch with the Soviet Government on behalf of Your Excellency
and it has no intention of doing so.

2.   Nippon Government would like to study separately as to the
possibility of Your Excellency's making political move towards India through
the Chungking Regime.

3.   Nippon Government desires that Your Excellency would endeavour
in bringing our active combined operations to a successful issue in spite
of present difficulty of war situations through good understanding of
Nippon's intention.

. . . . . .

30

"Netaji Alive" Even
If It Means He Has to
Be with the Communists

When the Communists were about to take over China's administration in the last quarter of 1949, adherents of Netaji and his near ones, felt comfortable to align Netaji with the Communists, the communists who once called him "Tojo's dog."

"Netaji is alive and with the Chinese Communists in Peking," read the daily newspaper 'Netajee' from New Delhi. They announced, *"he would broadcast over Peking Radio at 3.30 p.m. GMT on Oct. 21…on the 233-metre wavelength."*

The next day, 6 Oct. '49, Sarat Chandra Bose too expressed that the Govt of India was in possession of definite information that Subhas Chandra Bose is alive and *"with the Communists in China."* He however considered the report of the impending radio broadcast to be *"just a piece of sensational news cooked up somewhere."*

The above are not reports from the domestic newspaper of the day but from Hong Kong-based 'China Mail' of 6th and 8th Oct. 1949.

The belief that Netaji was still alive goes to show that people could not come to terms with the loss of Netaji in 1945.

The China Mail, 1949-10-06

Subhas Chandra Bose Said With Chinese Reds

New Delhi, October 5.

Subhas Chandra Bose, former leader of the wartime Indian National Army, is alive and with the Chinese Communists in Peking, the daily newspaper "Netajee" reported here today.

"Netajee," official organ of the "forward bloc" which was founded by Bose in 1940, said he would broadcast over Peking Radio at 3.30 p.m. GMT on October 21. The reports said the broadcast would be on the 233 metre wavelength.

Subhas Chandra Bose was reported killed when the Japanese bomber carrying him from Saigon to Tokyo crashed when taking off from a Formosa airfield on August 18, 1945. Since that time there had been persistent reports that he was not dead but had gone to Moscow and recently had joined up with the Chinese Communists.—United Press.

---

re than 30 anti- . . missing, ac- es received in ght.

ch usually plies d China's West l, left Macao

by more than at Shekpan, th West of the

dded that the ped of all goods ers robbed of personal pro- jewellery.

s carried out night.

e alongside the r boats. The rt were over- er of passengers

ners nghai

i, October 5. tates Consul- ew survey of in the Shang- rict, announced Americans are Yangtse valley Shanghai and

0 official per- the Consulate out 800 are in

line on wages and simultaneously lower the prices of some goods through subsidies.

It was reported a special session of the National Assembly would be called. A new government cannot be officially approved until the Assembly is in session.

Informed government quarters said it was possible that the 65-year-old Premier, who has headed the French government for more than a year, would only hand in the resignation of his cabinet. This would permit him to explain his position to the National Assembly before his government is put out of office.

It is debatable, however, if President Auriol would accept the resignation and leave France without a government at the most critical moment in its post-war history. Mr. Queuille's middle of the road government has ruled France since September 11, 1948 —the first to survive a full year in office since 1944.

It was reported that Mr. Queuille would go to Rambouillet, 40 miles outside of Paris, where President Auriol is resting.—Reuter and United Press.

FOLLOW THE FASHION

BY DRIVING A

that United or military— will largely attitude and alks between r and the

ink that the on his vital a test of th Mr. Nehru s they will India's policy the Truman owed anti-

mpromise

ure United th East Asia hether Pre- Pandit Nehru mise formula ndia and the s in working d programme ent Truman's

urvers say In nor the officially res- ial Premier, e's move for n Conference

t London and cognised that n programme and whole- n of India

AUSSIE REQUEST TO RUSSIA

Canberra, October 6.

The Australian Government has asked the Soviet Government to allow greater freedom of movement to Australian diplomats in Russia, Dr. Herbert Evatt, the Minister for External Affairs, announced today.

Dr. Evatt said that restrictions were placed on the movement of all the accredited representatives in Russia. The Australian Government was anxious that the same privileges and facilities which apply to Russian diplomats in Australia should apply to Australian diplomats in Russia.—Reuter.

ECCENTRIC WANTS TO BE PREMIER

Paris, October 6.

Ushers at the Elysees Palace, the residence of the President of the Republic, M. Vincent Auriol, today gently but firmly ejected Ferdinand Lop, a colourful Latin Quarter character, who wanted to offer his services as the new French Premier.

Lop, an eccentric who starts political arguments in cafes, has made the same offer several times before.

Today he commented that "only a man without political bias can save the country from ruin".—Reuter.

ment for its own capital, and machinery for foreign investment was cumbersome and slow-moving.

CHANDRA BOSE MYSTERY

Calcutta, October 6.

The Government of India has information that Subhas Chandra Bose is alive in Communist China, his elder brother, Sarat Chandra Bose, said today.

Interviewed while he lay sick in bed, Sarat Chandra Bose said: "I believe, as I have always believed, that Subhas is alive. The story of the air crash on Formosa in August, 1945, when was reported to have been killed has never really convinced me."

Sarat Bose he was aware that the Government of India was in possession of definite information that Subhas Chandra Bose is alive and with the Communists in China.

"This does not necessarily mean the report that he will broadcast over Peiping Radio on October 21 is true. I suspect this to be a fabrication based perhaps on the prediction of an Indian astrologer who visited New Delhi recently. It is just a piece of sensational news cooked up somewhere."—United Press.

Manila, October 6.

Two major roadblocs to renewed friendly relations between Japan and the Philippines were outlined today by the Chief of the Philippine Mission to Tokyo.

Minister Bernabe Africa told Manila Law College students it develops on Japan to restore friendly relations by:

First, meeting just obligations to the Philippines in the form of war indemnity payments.

Second, convincing the Filipinos of Japan's peaceful intentions.

Mr. Africa was appalled by the United States move stopping reparations payments to Allied countries. He described it as "a disaster to Allied convictions."

He said: "Condonation of reparations payments from Japan, when that country has only paid a pittance to those countries whom she destroyed and overran during the war, is not only against basic Allied policy towards Japan, but a definite encouragement to future aggression".—Associated Press.

Annecy, October, 6.

Exceptionally warm autumn weather in the Annecy region, in the French Alps, is making apple trees bloom for the second time this year.—Reuter.

Comm Far

Londo

Six general Lancasters from Force Coastal leave their Com November 1 for

They will tr operational and control of Air Ho East Air Force.

Each with a cre aircraft will carr cise in air mobili flying, and mari rance. The crew change views doctrine with k Air Force author

The Lancaster RAF station at pore, on Novemb ily out by way bahiyah (Iraq) tan), and Negom

Leaving Singap ber 29, they will wall, where the December 11, by bo, Karachi, Ade and Malta.—Reut

31

This Is How Misinformation Is Peddled by a Netaji Cult

A conspiracy theorist said:

"Sarat was Subhas Bose's elder brother and an eminent political leader. He passed away in 1950, knowing that his brother was alive and in China."

This is twisting of information.

The fact is, Sarat has never, himself, said that he knows that Subhas was alive and in China.

What Sarat said and what was reported is this:

The 'Nation' reported – *'Mr. Sarat Chandra Bose said here yesterday that the Government of India were in possession of definite information that Netaji Subhas Chandra Bose was in Red China of Mao Tse-Tung.'*

He further said –*'It is not possible for me to say where he (Netaji) is at the moment because I have no information myself. But as I have already said, I believe, and I have always believed that he is alive. It is futile to search for him.'*

It boils down simply to:

1. Sarat had no information on the whereabouts of his brother Subhas.

2. He believed that his brother was alive.

3. Govt. of India, and not he, was in possession of definite information that Subhas was in Red China (this apparently is a strategic statement/testing the water, to persuade Government for a reaction).

In conclusion, Sarat did not know where Subhas was, living or dead.

NETAJI ALIVE—BELIEVES SJ. SARAT BOSE

"He Would Appear Again In Appropriate Moment"

By A Staff Reporter

The belief that Netaji was alive was expressed by Sj. Sarat Chandra Bose addressing a public meeting in Calcutta on Thursday.

Sj. BOSE said that though he had no information of Netaji yet he had this belief that Netaji was alive and perhaps due to some reason best known to him he was not emerging from his secluded life.

It would be futile on their part, Sj. Bose said, to conduct any search for him or to try to secure any news of his present whereabouts. When proper time would come and when Netaji would think the moment appropriate for his emergence he would appear again and would come to his motherland to fulfil his unfinished task.

32

This Misperception
Needs to Be Corrected

An article (link is given below) published in 'DNA India' on 28 Oct. 2015 has this to say on Purabi Roy's work on Netaji mystery:

Prof. Sobhanlal Dutta Gupta, an internationally renowned Comintern and Gramsci scholar who was a member of a study team (the other was Purabi Roy), categorically stated that their "project had nothing to do with Netaji. It was a project to collect materials from the Russian archives between 1917 and 1947 concerning Indo-Russian relations. The two volumes published by the Asiatic Society bear evidence of that. Of course, if anything related to Bose was to be found, it would be included. But the papers, which we could access in 1995, did not contain any material on Bose. This misperception needs to be corrected."

It may be recollected that Purabi Roy failed to establish her 'Russian theory' claim in the Inquiry conducted by the Justice Mukherjee Commission (1999–2005). She could neither put up any documents from Russian archives in support of her claims nor did the witnesses she produced corroborate her statements. The set of papers she submitted in Russian to the Commission, on translation revealed nothing worthwhile.

https://www.dnaindia.com/analysis/column-quest-for-netaji-plagued-by-sensationalism-2139179?fbclid=IwAR2cSynAoR-hhHXz_2b5np3HhxcCXBrbTA0--0NdMNn25Q1L-bTj91g2vCc.

if afflicted with sensationalism. Sadly enough, some historians fail to insulate themselves from this ahistoric propensity. Professor Hari Sankar Vasudevan of the University of Calcutta said two years back that as a member of a three-member team, commissioned by the Asiatic Society of Calcutta, he worked at the Russian archives in the early 1990s in search of Netaji's fate. But Prof Sobhanlal Dutta Gupta, an internationally renowned Comintern and Gramsci scholar who was a member of the team (the other was Prof Roy), in a communication to this writer, categorically stated that the "project had nothing to do with Netaji. It was a project to collect materials from the Russian archives between 1917-1947 concerning Indo-Russian relations. The two volumes published by the Asiatic Society bear evidence of that. Of course, if anything related to Bose was to be found, it would be included. But the papers, which we could access in 1995, did not contain any material on Bose. This misperception needs to be corrected.

The media, unfortunately, gives in to sensationalism — for instance, despite a clear verdict that the handwriting and DNA test of Gumnami Baba did not tally with Netaji's, it continued with the stories. However, senior journalist Dhirendra K Jha furnished evidence that the Baba's photograph was a computer-generated and digitally enhanced image of Netaji. It was obviously meant to feed the fantasies of conspiracy theorists. Dr VN Arora, formerly principal of the Saket Degree College, Faizabad, and a journalist who too believed that the Baba was Netaji, found cartons of cigarettes and bottles of Scotch whisky when he visited Baba's room after his death. Netaji was never known to have been alcoholic. So Bose's spiritual transformation into Gumnami Baba was perhaps a myth. Roy who never bought the Baba theory rightly says, "Every account of history" should undergo a "clinical and unbiased" scrutiny.

33

RTI Reply by GoI

In an RTI (Right to Information) reply on 31 May 2017, Government of India restated "Netaji Died In 1945 Plane Crash."

News link is given below:

https://youtu.be/nULLSzMNPBI

34

What Came Out of
the Declassified Netaji Files

Here are the five most important facts that have emerged from the declassified Netaji files, www.netajipapers.gov.in:

1. DEATH OF BOSE

Dozens of conspiracy theories had surfaced not only on alternate mediums of information, but also carried by mainstream publications which claimed that Bose did not die in the plane crash in Taiwan, but had left to take a safe refuge in the Soviet Union or somewhere else.

However, the declassified Bose files reveal that he succumbed to the injuries suffered in the plane crash on August 18, 1945. His body was cremated 2 days later, and the ashes were carefully despatched to Tokyo.

Six Reports by the British, American and Jap Investigation Agencies, conducted soon after the incident in 1945, by interviewing eyewitnesses, concluded that Netaji succumbed to his injuries on 18 Aug. '45. The KGB, too, accepted the British find. Two Indian Inquiries conducted 11 and 25 years after the incident also concurred with the findings of the Investigative Agencies. The 1st Inquiry interviewed 11 eyewitnesses.

The 3rd Indian Inquiry held 55 years after the incident, could interview only 1 surviving 90+ aged eyewitness with fading memory. It found out that there is "no document in proof of the fact that there was any plane accident," and concluded that Netaji did not die in the plane crash. But the Commission could not say how else and where else did Netaji die. It rubbished both the Russian angle as well as the 'Baba' theories.

2. INA TREASURES

There is no clear information of the quantity and value of treasures that got boarded in the ill-fated plane in two 30″ sized suitcases. Estimates varied from Rs. 1 Lac to Rs. 1 Crore (1945 price) The only credible information came from Netaji's personal valet, Kundan Singh, who was present at the time when the boxes containing valuables were checked before Netaji's departure from Bangkok on 17 Aug. '45. He said the boxes contained jewellery, Pounds, Guineas and gold wires. What came back in 1951 (and identified by Kundan Singh) as materials salvaged from the Taihoku airport, via the Japanese and Netaji's associate Rammurty, was 11 kg of semi-charred pieces of jewellery, now resting in the National Museum.

Before departure from Bangkok on 17 Aug. '45, Netaji disposed the INA funds in the bank, through donations to Indo-Thai Committee, ex-gratia and advanced payments to INA staff. The British later confiscated some amount which was returned to the Indian Embassy in Thailand in 1950. The amount was utilised for educational purposes for Indians living there. The amounts recovered from Malaya and other Far Eastern stations were put in an 'Indian Relief Committee' Trust and utilised after independence for education purpose of Indian children in those countries.

3. BOSE'S IMMEDIATE FAMILY

The IB (Intelligence Bureau) was aware of the existence of Emilie Schenkl and Anita from 1943–44 when they intercepted Emelie's letter to Sarat Bose while he was under detention in Ooty. They were also aware of her later letter to Sarat Bose's daughter Sm

Chitra. Followed by further investigation in 1953 and verification of related records, the Government of India recognised Anita as the daughter of Subhas Ch Bose, on 8.6.54. The Congress Party thereafter took charge of assisting Anita till she attained the age of 18/marriage. Earlier to this, members of the Bose family were assisting them.

4. BOSE WAS NOT A 'WAR CRIMINAL'

Ministry of External Affairs had filed an enquiry with their British counterpart to ascertain whether Bose's name figure in the 'War Criminal' list as they had on several occasions reiterated that he was a traitor. The reply from the British side was: "Bose's name is not in the list of war criminals drawn up by the UK after World War II." Neither does Bose's name figure in the 'War Criminal' list drawn up by the UN.

5. BRINGING OF THE REMAINS FROM RENKOJI TEMPLE

Amidst pressure from many quarters and requests from the head priest of Renkoji temple, the Government did not eventually bring the ashes.

In 1971, Indira Gandhi feared that the return of Bose ashes would create panic among many of his supporters who firmly believed that he was alive.

A pressure for shifting the ashes to India came from old associates of Netaji in Japan, who were advancing in age and who felt a personal sense of responsibility of the ashes. This, coupled with Japan Government's query on any requirement by India to take over the ashes on the 50th anniversary of Netaji's death (1995) or the birth centenary (1997), Indian Government initiated a proposal of bringing the ashes on the occasion of Netaji's birth centenary. But both the Ministry of External Affairs and Home Ministry advised the Prime Minister to maintain a status quo in the absence of consensus among political parties. Instead of bringing the ashes, it was decided to increase maintenance fund sent to the temple authority for the safekeeping of the Netaji's remains.

Irrespective of the Party in power, GoI's stand has been, there is no political benefit in bringing the ashes.

35

World War II, Taihoku
Airfield and the Plane Crash

A detailed day-by-day listing of events during the 2nd World War, a database, recognised by the US Library of Congress, mentions Subhas Chandra Bose's death in a plane crash at Taihoku on 18 Aug. 1945 and all the subsequent related activities.

The timeline of the Taihoku (Matsuyama) airport, from 30 March 1936 to 16 April 1950, also lists the air crash that took place on 18 Aug. 1945 killing Subhas Chandra Bose *(image 1)*.

The Matsuyama Airfield was built in Taihoku in 1936. Bombers of Jap Navy's Air Group had based here for the purpose of bombing Chinese positions along the Chinese coast. The US Army Far East Air Forces bombed Matsuyama several times between Mar. and Aug. 1945, with the final mission taking place on 12 Aug. 1945, 6 days before Netaji's mishap. After the war, the airfield was renamed Songshan, a Chinese pronunciation of the Japanese Kanji-writing for Matsuyama. Songshan became a base of the Chinese Air Force in 1946. Beginning in 1950, it saw mixed military and civilian use, which would remain so through today. It is now the secondary civilian international airport serving the city of Taipei.

In the day-by-day timeline of events that occurred throughout the world, the database mentions:

On 18 Aug. 1945 *(image 2)*, against Taiwan, Subhas' death following an air crash at Taiwan, see enlarged view *(image 3)*.

On 20th Aug. 1945 *(image 4)*, against Taiwan, cremation of Subhas Bose, see enlarged view *(image 5)*.

On 23rd Aug. 1945 *(image 6)*, against Japan, "Japanese news agency Do Trzei announced the death of Subhas Chandra Bose."

On 7th Sept. 1945 *(image 7)*, against Japan, that Subhas Bose's ashes were brought to Tokyo by Lt. Tatsuo Hayashida.

On 8th Sept. 1945 *(image 8)*, against Japan, Rama Murti received Bose's ashes, in Tokyo.

On 14th Sept. 1945 *(image 9)*, against Japan, "A memorial for Subhas Chandra Bose was held in Tokyo."

Those who believe that Netaji died elsewhere and at some other time may put up a similar time-line with supporting verified documents.

Matsuyama Airfield Timeline

1

30 Mar 1936 Matsuyama Airfield in Taihoku (now Taipei), Taiwan began its operations.

1 Apr 1936 Japan Air Transport's Fukuoka-Naha-Taihoku air route began, transporting passengers between southern Japan, Okinawa, and Taiwan.

23 Feb 1938 40 SB bombers of the Soviet Volunteer Group of the Chinese Air Force took off from Hankou, Hubei Province, China (28 bombers, all Soviet crews) and Nanchang, Jiangxi Province, China (12 bombers, mixed Soviet and Chinese crews) to attack Matsuyama Airfield in Taihoku (now Taipei), Taiwan. Only the 28 bombers from Hankou reached the target area; those from Nanchang turned back after failing to identify the target due to cloud cover. Having arrived without being detected, the crews turned off their engines and glided with stealth, releasing over 200 bombs at high altitude. The crews reported 40 Japanese aircraft destroyed on the group, while Japanese reports noted 12 aircraft destroyed. A number of hangars and fuel tanks were also destroyed or damaged. Song Meiling (Madam Chiang Kaishek) hosted a victory banquet after the Soviet airmen returned to China.

12 Oct 1944 Carrier aircraft from USS Bunker Hill attacked Matsuyama Airfield in Taihoku (now Taipei), Taiwan.

23 Oct 1944 A Japanese passenger transport plane that had just taken off from Matsuyama Airfield (now Songshan Airport) in Taihoku (now Taipei), Taiwan lost control and crashed atop the mountain where the Taiwan Grand Shrine was located. The accident and resulting fires destroyed the Torii ceremonial archway, stone toro lanterns, and other structures.

2 Mar 1945 US B-24, B-25, and A-20 aircraft attacked Matsuyama Airfield in Taihoku (now Taipei), Taiwan.

12 Apr 1945 Avenger aircraft from HMS Victorious attacked Matsuyama Airfield in Taihoku (now Taipei) and shipping off Tamsui in northern Taiwan; Sub-Lieutenant Daniel McAleese was shot down, rescued, but would later die of his wounds.

13 Apr 1945 Avenger aircraft from HMS Victorious attacked Matsuyama Arifield in Taihoku (now Taipei), Taiwan, damaging runways, and barracks; one ammunition dump or oil storage tank exploded.

16 Apr 1945 US B-24 and P-51 aircraft attacked Matsuyama Airfield in Taihoku (now Taipei), Taiwan.

5 May 1945 US B-25 bombers attacked Matsuyama Airfield in Taihoku (now Taipei), Taiwan.

6 May 1945 US B-24 bombers attacked Matsuyama Airfield in Taihoku (now Taipei), Taiwan.

17 May 1945 B-24 bombers of US 380th Bomb Group attacked Matsuyama Airfield in Taihoku (now Taipei), Taiwan.

7 Jul 1945 US B-24 bombers attacked Matsuyama Airfield in Taihoku (now Taipei), Taiwan.

18 Jul 1945 US B-24 bombers attacked Matsuyama Airfield in Taihoku (now Taipei), Taiwan.

9 Aug 1945 US B-24 bombers attacked Matsuyama Airfield in Taihoku (now Taipei), Taiwan.

12 Aug 1945 US B-24 bombers from Okinawa, Japan attacked Matsuyama Airfield in Taihoku (now Taipei), Taiwan.

18 Aug 1945 Subhash Chandra Bose boarded a Japanese passenger aircraft at Matsuyama Airfield (now Songshan Airport) at Taihoku (now Taipei), Taiwan for a trip to Japan. The aircraft crashed immediately after takeoff and Bose was seriously burned. He was rushed to a military hospital near the airfield, but the doctors were not able to save him.

5 Sep 1945 USMC Major Dick Johnson, flying a TBM-3 Avenger aircraft, landed at Matsuyama Airfield in Taihoku (now Taipei), Taiwan. He was the first US airman to arrive on Taiwan after the cease of hostilities.

16 Apr 1950 Songshan Airport in Taipei, Taiwan began serving civilian traffic.

2

- Americans began parachuting medical and aid teams into selected prisoners of war camps in the Japanese Home Islands. [AC]
- Soviet First Deputy Commissar for Foreign Affairs Andrei Vyshinsky submitted a list of names of Germans who could be sent to the Nuremberg Trials to his superior Vyacheslav Molotov. The list consisted of Ferdinand Schörner, Hans Fritzsche, HansGünch Voß, Adolf Beckerle, and Rainer Stahel. [Main Article | CPC]

China

- Nearly 4,000 Japanese troops surrendered along the Hailar River in Liaobei Province, China, effectively ending organised resistance. [Main Article | AC, CPC]
- Guo Fengwu, the deputy commander of the 24th Pursuit Squadron of the Chinese Air Force, flew over Guisui, Suiyuan (now Hohhot, Inner Mongolia), China and dropped leaflets containing a transcript of Emperor Shōwa's 15 Aug 1945 radio address. He was shot down by Japanese anti-aircraft fire and became the final Chinese Air Force casualty of the war. [Main Article | CPC]
- The Eastern Mongolian Branch of the Inner Mongolian People's Revolutionary Party, based in the town of Wangin (now Ulan Hot), Xing'an Province, China and consisted of several bureaucrats of the former puppet nation Manchukuo, declared Inner Mongolia a part of the secessionist Mongolian People's Republic. [CPC]
- In Chongqing, China, French and Chinese representatives signed a document that officially returned Kouang-Tchéou-Wan (Chinese: Guangzhouwan) back to China. This treaty port had been forcibly leased by Qing Dynasty China to France in Nov 1899, who placed it under the administration of French Indochina. [CPC]

Dutch East Indies

- The Preparatory Committee for the Independence of Indonesia endorsed the constitution drafted in Jun 1945, though with two changes. The special position for Islam was deleted, and the office of the president received virtually dictatorial powers for the transitional period before a legislative assembly could be elected. Sukarno and Mohammad Hatta was named the President and Vice President of the new republic. [CPC]

Hong Kong

- Chinese communist rebels attacked the Japanese garrison in Hong Kong, hoping to take control of the port city before either the Chinese Nationalist government or the British colonial administration took it; the Japanese successfully repulsed the communist attack. [CPC]

Japan

- The last air conflict of WW2 took place over Tokyo, Japan. Two US reconnaissance aircraft were attacked by fighters and flak. One American crewman was killed and two fighters were shot down. [AC]
- Soviet troops landed on Paramushiro, Kurile Islands, Japan. [Main Article | CPC]
- The Japanese Home Ministry secretly sent radio messages to local police chiefs, ordering them to organize comfort woman facilities for incoming US occupation troops as an attempt to safeguard Japanese women. On this topic, Prince Fumimaro Konoe told the national police commissioner "Please defend the young women of Japan". [Main Article | CPC]

Philippines

- The British fleet carrying bureaucrats and troops for Hong Kong reached the Philippine Islands. [CPC]

Singapore

- At the headquarters of the Japanese 7th Area Army in Singapore, General Seishiro Itagaki informed his lieutenants and colonial administrators that Japan had surrendered. He ordered the men to maintain public order and to plan for the transition of power when the British colonial administration would arrive. He also ordered the construction of an internment camp in Jurong in western Singapore for Japanese civilians, who would wait there until repatriation. [Main Article | Event | CPC]

Taiwan

- Subhash Chandra Bose boarded a Japanese passenger aircraft at Matsuyama Airfield (now Songshan Airport) at Taihoku (now Taipei), Taiwan for a trip to Japan. The aircraft crashed immediately after takeoff and Bose was seriously burned. He was rushed to a military hospital near the airfield, but the doctors were not able to save him. [Main Article | Facility | CPC]

Hong Kong

3

- Chinese communist rebels attacked the Japanese garrison in Hong Kong, hoping to take control of the port city before either the Chinese Nationalist government or the British colonial administration took it; the Japanese successfully repulsed the communist attack. [CPC]

Japan

- The last air conflict of WW2 took place over Tokyo, Japan. Two US reconnaissance aircraft were attacked by fighters and flak. One American crewman was killed and two fighters were shot down. [**AC**]
- Soviet troops landed on Paramushiro, Kurile Islands, Japan. [**Main Article** | CPC]
- The Japanese Home Ministry secretly sent radio messages to local police chiefs, ordering them to organize comfort women facilities for incoming US occupation troops as an attempt to safeguard Japanese women. On this topic, Prince Fumimaro Konoe told the national police commissioner "Please defend the young women of Japan". [**Main Article** | CPC]

Philippines

- The British fleet carrying bureaucrats and troops for Hong Kong reached the Philippine Islands. [CPC]

Singapore

- At the headquarters of the Japanese 7th Area Army in Singapore, General Seishiro Itagaki informed his lieutenants and colonial administrators that Japan had surrendered. He ordered the men to maintain public order and to plan for the transition of power when the British colonial administration would arrive. He also ordered the construction of an internment camp in Jurong in western Singapore for Japanese civilians, who would wait there until repatriation. [**Main Article** | **Event** | CPC]

Taiwan

- Subhash Chandra Bose boarded a Japanese passenger aircraft at Matsuyama Airfield (now Songshan Airport) at Taihoku (now Taipei), Taiwan for a trip to Japan. The aircraft crashed immediately after takeoff and Bose was seriously burned. He was rushed to a military hospital near the airfield, but the doctors were not able to save him. [**Main Article** | **Facility** | CPC]

20 Aug 1945

<u>**4**</u>

China

- Soviet forces declared the cities of Mukden (Liaoning Province), Changchun (Jilin Province), and Qiqihar (Nenjiang Province) in northeastern China secure. [Main Article | CPC]
- He Yingqin arrived in Zhijiang, Hunan Province, China and met with China Expeditionary Army representative Takeo Imai to negotiate surrender terms. [Main Article | CPC]
- The final naval engagement of WW2 took place along the Chinese coast between Wenzhou and Shanghai between a Japanese-manned junk equipped with a howitzer and two smaller Sino-American junks each equipped with a bazooka (five rounds each) and various small arms. The Allies were of the US Navy Sino-American Special Technical Cooperative Organization (SACO) organization. The Japanese junk surrendered after 44 of its 83-men crew were killed; 35 were wounded. 4 Chinese were killed on the Allied side; 4 Chinese and 1 American were wounded. This was also the last US Navy engagement in a vessel powered by sail. [CPC]

Dutch East Indies

- The leadership of the newly created Republic of Indonesia decided to form the Badan Keamanan Rakjat, or the People's Security Organization, which was to become its army. [CPC]

French Indochina

- Emperor Bao Dai of Vietnam sent messages to Allied leaders, urging them to recall the returning French colonial administration. In the message to Charles de Gaulle, he noted "You would understand better if you could see what is happening here, if you could feel this desire for independence which is in everyone's heart.... Even if you come to re-establish a French administration here, it will no longer be obeyed; each village will be a nest of resistance, each former collaborator an enemy, and your officials and colonists will themselves ask to leave this atmosphere which they will be unable to breathe." [Main Article | CPC]
- In Thai Nguyen, Tonkin, French Indochina, communist leader Vo Nguyen Giap disrupted a previously peaceful Vietnamese-Japanese transfer of power negotiation by ordering his Viet Minh troops to fire on the Japanese personnel. The Japanese fell back into the building and became besieged. Meanwhile, to the south in Hanoi, the Viet Minh began to consolidate its recently gained power over Hanoi by massacring Dai Viet supporters and broadcasting pro-communist/anti-French propaganda. [CPC]
- Chinese occupation troops began moving into Tonkin, French Indochina. They met some resistance from Viet Minh personnel in the upper Red River region. [CPC]
- Laotian nationalist groups Lao Issara and Lao-pen-Lao took control of Savannakhet and Thakhek ahead of the incoming Chinese occupation forces and French colonial administrators. [CPC]

Pacific Ocean

- I-401 received orders to report in with her current location. Tatsunosuke Ariizumi, commanding officer of 6th Fleet who was aboard the submarine, did not respond. [Main Article | CPC]

Russia

- Joseph Stalin signed the final GKO order (No. 9887) making Lavrentiy Beria the head of State Committees No. 1 (atomic research), No. 2 (jet engine research), and No. 3 (radio location equipment development); he no longer held direct authority over counterintelligence. [Main Article | CPC]
- Pavel Meshik was named the deputy head of the Soviet 1st Main Directorate for the construction of atomic weapons. [CPC]

Singapore

- The Singapore-based Japanese newspaper Syonan Shimbun announced the surrender and reproduced the transcript of the Imperial Rescript. [CPC]

Taiwan

- Subhash Chandra Bose was cremated in the main crematorium of Taihoku (now Taipei), Taiwan. [Main Article | CPC]

United Kingdom

- Percy Hobart's British 79th (Experimental) Armoured Division Royal Engineers was disbanded. [CPC]
- British Foreign Minister Ernest Bevin announced to the Parliament that the treatment of Thailand would depend on

Pacific Ocean   **5**

- I-401 received orders to report in with her current location. Tatsunosuke Ariizumi, commanding officer of 6th Fleet who was aboard the submarine, did not respond. [**Main Article** | CPC]

Russia

- Joseph Stalin signed the final GKO order (No. 9887) making Lavrentiy Beria the head of State Committees No. 1 (atomic research), No. 2 (jet engine research), and No. 3 (radio location equipment development); he no longer held direct authority over counterintelligence. [**Main Article** | CPC]
- Pavel Meshik was named the deputy head of the Soviet 1st Main Directorate for the construction of atomic weapons. [CPC]

Singapore

- The Singapore-based Japanese newspaper Syonan Shimbun announced the surrender and reproduced the transcript of the Imperial Rescript. [CPC]

Taiwan

- Subhash Chandra Bose was cremated in the main crematorium of Taihoku (now Taipei), Taiwan. [**Main Article** | CPC]

United Kingdom

- Percy Hobart's British 79th (Experimental) Armoured Division Royal Engineers was disbanded. [CPC]
- British Foreign Minister Ernest Bevin announced to the Parliament that the treatment of Thailand would depend on Thailand's willingness to cooperate with Allied authorities and its willingness to rebuild the entire region's economy. [**Main Article** | CPC]

23 Aug 1945   **6**

- Douglas MacArthur ordered 5,000 Filipino internees in Manila, Philippine Islands freed. [**Main Article** | CPC]
- A new British colonial administration departed Colombo, Ceylon for Singapore. [CPC]
- The United Kingdom ratified the United Nations Charter. [CPC]
- The Soviet Union announced that all Japanese resistance in the Manchuria region of northeastern China had ceased. Meanwhile, Soviet troops received the surrender of the Japanese garrison at Paramushiro, Kurile Islands. [**Main Article** | CPC]
- Douglas MacArthur ordered the release of all Filipinos, most of whom Japanese collaborators, who were interned by the US Army. He noted that their fates would be tried by the Filipino government, not by the US military. [**Main Article** | CPC]

China

- He Yingqin ordered Japanese generals in northern and eastern China to continue to maintain peace until Nationalist forces would arrive to relieve them. [**Main Article** | **Event** | CPC]
- The Chinese communists declared the slogan "peace, democracy, and unification", which conveyed the message of cooperation with the Nationalist government. The real intention, however, was to curry favor from the Americans, while buying time to strengthen its military and political positions. [CPC]

French Indochina

- In the morning, Viet Minh forces took took control of Hue, Annam, French Indochina. In the afternoon, Viet Minh leadership organized a demonstration to legitimize the takeover; this was participated by minor figures in the royal family. Although the demonstrated refrained from entering the palace, they nevertheless caused Emperor Bao Dai to consider abdication. At the same time, Viet Minh personnel arrested former premier Pham Quynh and former minister Ngo Dinh Khoi and his son. [**Main Article** | CPC]
- Tran Trong Kim stepped down as the Prime Minister of the Empire of Vietnam. [**Main Article** | CPC]

Guam

- USS Sterlet arrived at Midway, ending her fifth war patrol. [**Main Article** | **Facility** | CPC]

Japan

- USS Yorktown (Essex-class) received orders to operate east of Honshu, Japan and provide cover for the forces occupying Japan. [**Main Article** | **Event** | **DS**]
- Japanese news agency Do Trzei announced the death of Subhash Chandra Bose. [**Main Article** | CPC]

US Pacific Islands

7 Sep 1945

- USS Sea Cat arrived at Guam, Mariana Islands. [**Main Article** | CPC]
- The Allies held a victory parade was held in Berlin, Germany. [CPC]
- Australia ratified the United Nations Charter. [CPC]

Australian New Guinea

- Allied prisoners of war at Rabaul, New Britain, technically freed on 16 Aug 1945 but still remained under Japanese care, were liberated by men under Royal Australian Navy Captain P. Brice Morris. [CPC]

China

- Chinese General Zhang Fakui and his troops entered Guangzhou, Guangdong Province, China. [CPC]
- General Tang Enbo arrived in Shanghai, China with the mission to ensure peace, stability, and Nationalist control in the Nanjing-Shanghai region. [CPC]

Japan

- Subhash Chandra Bose's ashes were brought to Tokyo, Japan by Lieutenant Tatsuo Hayashida. [**Main Article** | CPC]

Taiwan

- Chinese leadership in Taiwan abolished all orders given by the Japanese administration. [CPC]

United Kingdom

- A Monetary Agreement was signed by the governments of the United Kingdom and the Netherlands in London, England, United Kingdom. [CPC]

8 Sep 1945

China

- Escorted by eight fighters, He Yingqin arrived in Nanjing, China by air at 0900 hours; later in the day he would meet with General Yasuji Okamura to work out the surrender ceremony details. [**Main Article** | **Event** | CPC]
- Chinese troops took control of Yueyang, Hunan Province and Kaifeng, Henan Province, China. [CPC]
- Nationalist Chinese troops counterattacked against a Communist offensive in Tunliu County, Shanxi Province, China, causing more than 1,000 casualties on the Communist side. [CPC]
- The Chinese legislature reformed land tax exemption laws, which was to be carried out by provincial and city governments. [CPC]

Japan

- General Douglas MacArthur arrived in Tokyo, Japan. [**Main Article** | **Event** | TH]
- The Japanese Navy Northern Fleet surrendered to the Americans at Mutsu Bay, Japan. [**Main Article** | CPC]
- Former Japanese Prime Minister Hideki Tojo failed in his suicide attempt at Sugamo Prison, Tokyo, Japan. [**Main Article** | CPC]
- Elements of the USAAF 3rd Bomberment Group was assigned to Atsugi Airfield in Japan. [**Main Article** | CPC]
- Rama Murti, president of the Tokyo Indian Independence League, received Subhash Chandra Bose's ashes in Tokyo, Japan. [**Main Article** | CPC]

Korea

- American troops landed at Inchon, Korea to prevent the Soviet Union from breaking the previous agreement for Soviet troops to only occupy northern Korea. [**Main Article** | CPC]

Nauru

- Royal New Zealand Air Force aircraft dropped leaflets on Nauru and Ocean Islands, urging Japanese soldiers to stop fighting and surrender. [**Main Article** | CPC]

Russia

- Aleksandr Vasilevsky was made a Hero of the Soviet Union for the second time. [**Main Article** | CPC]

Japan

- A memorial for Subhash Chandra Bose was held in Tokyo, Japan. [**Main Article** | CPC]

Panama Canal Zone

- USS Whale arrived at the Panama Canal Zone. [**Main Article** | CPC]

United States

- USS San Diego arrived at Mare Island Naval Shipyard, Vallejo, California, United States for a scheduled overhaul. [**Main Article** | **Facility** | CPC]
- USS R-5 was decommissioned from service at Portsmouth, New Hampshire, United States. [**Main Article** | CPC]

36

The Last Journey
(Collected From Verified Sources)

The Americans dropped nuclear bombs on 6th, and 9th August 1945 and the Soviets declared war on Japan on August 10th. All calculations got upset, and Japan surrendered to the Allies on 15th August 1945.

Netaji was on a visit in Malaya when he got the shattering news of Japan's surrender. He received the news in a calm and even manner: "So that is that. Now, what next?"

Japan's surrender was not India's surrender. Netaji returned to Singapore immediately and held a series of meetings with his officers and advisers for a whole day and night. With the INA severely battered after the defeat in Burma, he decided to surrender with his troops at Singapore. But he was persuaded to take the help of the Japanese who offered to take him further east so that he does not fall into the hands of the Anglo-Americans.

On 16th August '45 afternoon, Netaji reached Bangkok. The Japanese Minister to the PGAH (Provisional Government of Azad Hind) officially conveyed Japan's decision to surrender and offered Netaji of any assistance from the Government of Japan. In response, Netaji told him that since Japan has surrendered unconditionally, they would not be in a position to provide any protection to him. Netaji expressed his desire to go to the Soviet land.

There was no time to contact the Soviets. Soviets were also at war with Japan. He preferred his team to be a prisoner of the Soviets. And then, after establishing their bonafides as fighters for India's freedom, would secure Russian assistance for his objective. The modalities were uncertain but the objective fixed; "an adventure into the unknown."

At Bangkok, he made quick decisions. General Bhonsle was handed over the command of the INA. A committee was formed to look after the affairs of the IIL (Indian Independence League). From the 'Treasures' large donations were made to Hospital, University, Indian Association, Thai-Bharat Cultural Lodge and others. All officers and staff were paid 2 to 3 months of advance payment.

Netaji chose Col. Habibur Rehman, Col. Gulzara Singh, Col. Pritam Singh, Major Abid Hasan, Debnath Das and SA Ayer to fly with him from Bangkok. They all vaguely knew that they were going to Manchuria. The Japanese arranged 2 planes to take them to Saigon, along with other Japanese personnel.

On 17th August early morning, the team left Bangkok for Saigon along with 2 large suitcases, about 3′ long, containing gold ornaments and other valuables and other smaller suitcases containing Netaji's personal kit.

The plane landed at Saigon the same morning. The team took rest in the town and had lunch. But things didn't work as per expectation. The Jap field unit was in utter confusion following the surrender. No plane was available to carry Netaji and his team. He was told that only one seat is available in a plane that was leaving Saigon the same day. And Netaji should take that seat as he is required to reach Tokyo at the earliest. Netaji refused the offer and insisted that his entire party of seven should move with him. On further consideration, one additional seat was offered. The Japs explained that the Allies had restricted their air travel and they are not sure whether airplane would be available in the future. They advised Netaji to accept the 2 seats. Netaji reluctantly accepted the 2-seat offer but on condition that the rest should be transported the following day. He chose Habibur Rehman to accompany him as he was in close touch with Netaji for a long time and was a senior member.

On arrival at the airport with their luggage, Netaji was told by the Chief Pilot that his baggage was too heavy for the already overloaded plane. Netaji refused to travel without the 2 leather suitcases containing gold and pieces of jewellery and despite the objection loaded them into the plane. He discarded some items from his personal kit instead. Netaji bade goodbye to all those who had come to see him. That was the last time his followers saw him.

The plane took off from Saigon at 5–5.30 in the evening of 17th with 12 or 13 on board; Netaji, Habibur and the rest Japanese. The pilot decided to halt for the night at Tourane, a couple of hours journey from Saigon. Netaji and other officers spent the night in a Hotel in the town. During this stay, the pilots made the plane lighter by unloading 12 antiaircraft machine guns and all ammunition.

At about 5 a.m. next day, 18th August, the plane took off for Taihoku. While on the way, they got information that Russians were advancing fast and the team's reaching Manchuria before the Russians occupied it has become doubtful. The plane landed at Taihoku at mid-day. All the passengers had lunch and rested at the airport while the ground engineer and co-pilot attended to a defect in the engine. After getting satisfied with its airworthiness, the team boarded the plane.

The plane took off from Taihoku at 2–2.30 p.m. on the 18th. The take-off was not quite normal. The plane made a steep ascent. Hardly had it reached a height of 30–40 m, there was a loud explosion, and the plane tilted to the left. The propeller and the port engine fell off. The plane nosedived and crashed to the ground 100 m beyond the concrete runaway, broke into two and the front portion immediately caught fire.

The crash affected different persons differently. 7 persons ultimately survived with various degrees of injuries. Netaji was splashed all over with petrol, but he had to rush out through the fire. Habibur followed him. Netaji's clothes and his entire body caught fire. Once outside, Habibur moved him away from the plane and took off Netaji's clothes with great difficulty and laid him down on the ground. Major Takashi, one of the survivors, made Netaji roll on the ground to put out the fire. Netaji's body and face were scorched with heat and his hairs singed. Habibur's hands and right side of the face were burnt, but his clothes did not catch fire. He too lay by Netaji's side.

Shortly afterwards, Netaji, along with other injured persons, was taken to a small military hospital nearby, rather a first-aid treatment centre. Among all the injured admitted, Netaji's condition was most serious. He was burnt all over, and his skin had taken a greyish colour like ash. His heart, too had burns. His face and eyes were swollen. His burns were of the severest type; third-degree. He had high fever, but surprisingly, he was in his senses. The CMO Dr. Yoshimi opined that Netaji was not likely to survive till the next morning. An ointment was applied all over the body, burns were dressed up and bandaged all over. 3 intravenous injections were given, and 6 other injections for his heart. Some blood from his body was let out and a blood transfusion given. Netaji was conscious at the beginning, so an interpreter was called to assist Netaji to speak to the Japanese personnel if desired. At 7–7.30 p.m. Netaji's condition deteriorated. In spite of administering stimulants, his heart and pulse beat did not improve. Slowly his life ebbed away. He breathed his last shortly after 8 p.m. Dr. Yoshimi made out a medical certificate of his death writing his name as 'Chandra Bose' In Japanese. Dr. Yoshimi, Dr. Tsuruta, 2 nurses, Mr. Nakamura the interpreter, Habibur Rehman and one military policeman was by his bedside at the time of his death. Immediately after Netaji passed away, the Japanese stood up and paid respect to his body by saluting. Habibur knelt by Netaji's bed and prayed.

With communications in shambles and amidst utter confusion in the ranks and files of the Japanese, the local authorities avoided taking responsibility of recording or declaring the death of the leader of a foreign friendly nation. The death certificate bore the name of Ichiro Okura who was cremated on 22nd August. But Habibur's and Nakamura's deposition to Shahnawaz Committee and other records say that Netaji was cremated on 20th August 1945. The ashes were collected the following day in a wooden urn and kept at Nishi Honganji Temple at Taihoku. A funeral ceremony was held in the Temple on 26/27 August. Later, on 6th September, Habibur was put on a plane to carry the urn to Tokyo. Habibur was also given a wooden box $3' \times 2\frac{1}{2}' \times 2'$, containing gold and jewellery retrieved from the airfield.

The official Japanese Radio announcement on Netaji's death was made on the 23rd. The news spread all over the globe. Indians were dumbstruck with the tragic news. A 'hartal' was observed on 24th August all over India. 'Subhas Day' was observed on the 25th. But to many, the death was unbelievable. They took it as yet another deception move by Netaji to escape from the clutches of the Allies.

The Allied Forces too did not believe the news at first. They instructed the Japs to submit a report on the news of Netaji's death. The Japs submitted their report on 19.9.45 confirming Netaji's death in the crash on 18.8.45.

The British Indian Govt sent Finney and Davis to SE Asia to investigate, and they too confirmed in Sept. '45 Netaji's death.

The Allied Forces conducted a detailed investigation under Col. Figges, and he submitted his Report on 25.7.46 stating "It is confirmed for certain that SC Bose died…on 18/08/1945"

Another investigation by Turner submitted on 19.10.46 reported the same news on Netaji's death to the Allies.

The Japs undertook a detailed investigation in 1955 and came to the same conclusion through their Report dated 13.12.55 making it certain that Netaji indeed died on 18.8.1945.

The link to Vasundhara TV article is given below:

http://vasundharatv.com/2017/08/20/india/last-journey-collected-verified-sources/?fbclid=IwAR1KRF09HChOhZ_qdWfzaqJQtVDCB75AL0mXKAeaxnOkvneSoj7GV3qf4tk.